GW00392508

BOSKENNA
& the PAYNTERS

by
Jim Hosking

'Ystorer Trevow' *(Historian of Villages)*

THE FORTUNES
OF A
CORNISH FAMILY
FROM 1670

Published by J.M. Hosking 1999

Pentreath, 9 Tredarvah Drive, Penzance, Cornwall UK TR18 4SU

E-mail: jim@tredarvah.free-online.co.uk

ISBN 0 9501296 4 X   © J.M. Hosking

Printed by Headland Printers Ltd., Penzance, Cornwall

Cover picture - Betty Paynter presented at Court, with her Parents

CONTENTS

pictures. Gilbert Evans and Florence. 'The connection' by David Evans. Capt. Gilbert Evans - Col. Paynter's agent. His diary 1909. No Popery. Mary Ann Care dies. Richard Richards= Mary Ann = Henry Care, family history. Your country needs you! 1914-1918. Buryan Races and Denmark. A fox as a visitor. Public duties. Mrs. Paynter dies.

Famous visitors. Marconi of wireless fame. Elettra. Romance. Mediterranean Cruise. Friends. Marconi's Parrot. Betty Presented at Court. Prince of Siam. Graham-white aviator. Recollections of David Evans. Miss Betty's Wedding Day. George Aukett retires. The honeymoon. Boskenna Deux.

Betty comes home. Wartime at Boskenna. Stephen Paull Jewell Hill. Childhood memories of David Evans. Like a Beetle. Fires at Boskenna. More ghosts. Betty remarries. Death of Col. Paynter.

Ibiza. Battle of Lamorna. Public Inquiry. 1957 Selling Boskenna Estate. Sale of Furniture and Antiques. Betty dies, 1980. Sonya.

APPENDIX

The Captain and Nellie (verse). The Staff at Boskenna. Mary Ann Care's family. 'Boskenna', some verses from a poem of 1868. Once upon a time.

ACKNOWLEDGEMENTS AND THANKS

BIBLIOGRAPHY

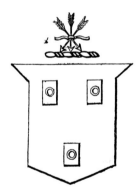

FOREWORD

THIS long-awaited story of the Paynter family, and of Boskenna Manor and estate, will rekindle memories in the minds and hearts of many in Cornwall and beyond,

That it is written by a St Buryan man, born and bred, who mingles pride in his subject with a genuine understanding and sympathy, makes it all the more appreciated.

A Cornish Bard, aptly titled 'Ystorer Trevow' (Historian of Villages), Jim Hosking tells this story of life down the generations and centuries with accuracy and affection: it is the result of many years of research and deep interest.

My memories of the family, sadly, encompass only the final years. In 1956, as a young journalist, I went to Boskenna to learn from the former Miss Betty Paynter (Mrs Paull Hill) that the estate was to be sold.

"I cannot afford to live here any longer," she said. Sitting in the Queen Anne library, and clearly distressed, she told me: "I would prefer someone to buy it who would live in it and love it as much as we have done."

Even that library had a history of its own: the walls were panelled from the wreck of a Spanish ship which was part of the Armada Fleet and had ended on the rocky coast nearby. A judge held court here; a small door on either side brought prisoners before him and gave them exit after trial.

She said the Paynter family could be traced to Boskenna from 1326, but from stones that had been recovered there was a genuine reason to believe there was a building here in Saxon times.

The following year the auction sale of antique furniture, pictures and effects was held in the drawing room at Boskenna: these family treasures were "going for a song" by today's prices. So were the farms and cottages when they were auctioned off in Penzance.

It was said that Colonel Paynter's most endearing characteristic was his ever-youthful capacity for enjoyment. That trait was inherited in full by his daughter, Betty, and retained despite the adversities in life that would have overwhelmed anyone less courageous.

Many years later, at her home in Penzance, she talked at length to me, in her deliciously entertaining style, of the highlights of her life, many of them recorded here by Mr Hosking.

She spoke of her friendships with many who came as guests at Boskenna, of the 'courtship' by Marconi, of the international personalties including the physicist Albert Einstein, whose Theory of Relativity was explained to her.

"I used to go boringly up to him and say 'Oh, Mr Einstein, I've forgotten what you said', and he used to start all over again."

There were two family ghosts. "We had Anne Paynter, who wanted to marry one of the tenants. They got the Press Gang to take him away and she went down to St Loy and drowned herself. She was seen frequently in the house by many people.

The other one was the man who walked up the back-drive carrying his head under his arm, and if he saw anybody he threw it at them, and they were dead within the year!"

An exuberance and a love of life lead to Mrs Paynter being the first woman to speak direct to Australia over the air from Marconi's transmitter at Poldhu, and to Miss Betty being the first woman to land in an aeroplane at the Isles of Scilly. The author has captured much of that family spirit of adventure, of the unexpected and the innovative, in this carefully prepared record.

DOUGLAS WILLIAMS M.B.E.

"Lef ha Pluven"   (Voice and Pen)

. . . .

FAMILY 'TREE' of PAYNTERS of BOSKENNA Part 1

William Paynter = Elinor Wilton = William Camborn alias Paynter

David   **Margaret**   **William**   **GEORGE CAMBORN** alias **PAYNTER**
b 1550   = Alice   of Deverill
shipwreckcd 1580 at   Courtney of   = Ann Antron
Pembroke with 3 sons, Penkevil   (Boskenna Paynters direct line in capitals)
settled in Wales.
Some desc. St.Ives

William Camborn alias **Paynter** **ARTHUR PAYNTER**   Jenkin Keigwin d 1595
= 1602 Loveday Courtney   of St. Erth d 1630
(ancestors of Rachel)   =(2) Joan Hawys   Richard Keigwin d 1636

Richard Paynter

William of Tremearne   **WILLIAM PAYNTER** = Jane Keigwin of Mousehole
               of Trelissick d 1681

Arthur = Mary Praed **William** (2)Margaret Pawlett =**1st FRANCIS** = (1) Suther land
d 1679   d 1715   1639-1724
                               of Boskenna

Francis =Margaret **Thomas** **Mary** **Arthur** **2nd FRANCIS** **Diana**   **James**
m 1706   = Thos.Haweis   1676-1762
  Mary = John Hearle   =1713 Mary Hawkey of Colan d1763

Betty Hearle   **Harriet Hearle** **Jane Hearle** **3rd FRANCIS** **Mary**   **Margaret**
= Capt.Wallis   = Rev.Henry   = Francis   1716-1775   b1719   b 1723
(discovered   Hawkins   Hearle   = Mary   = Samuel = Benjamin
Tahiti)   Tremayne   Rodd   Gully   Thomas   Pender
           of Heligan   of Trebartha

Chapter 1

EARLY BOSKENNA AND ITS OWNERS

Of those who lived there long ago
Some stories now are told
Of nine generations of Paynters
Way back in days of old.

If you stand near the celtic cross (Boskenna Cross) at the fork 1 mile south east of St. Buryan Churchtown, you will see that the land slopes gently away towards the sea at St.Loy and St.Dellan. Less than a mile to the east is Lamorna and to the west is Penberth in West Cornwall.

Nestling inland above St. Loy Bay, but nowadays surrounded by trees, lies the ancient seat of the Paynters.

The house itself is approached through two large granite-pillared gateposts and a driveway lined with blue hydrangeas and matured trees, which gives way to a grassy slope and lawns surrounding the present-day manor house.

This house, altered and rebuilt many times was home to various landed families of the parish who lived there before the Paynters.

The earliest house was, no doubt, a much more modest affair of natural granite stonework. It may indeed have had a thatched roof, and would have resembled the more low-built farmhouses that made up the majority of such holdings in this far western parish of St.Buryan.

No doubt the original buildings, long since disappeared, took the full force of a South easterly gale until the first Francis Paynter of Boskenna decided to plant trees to provide some shelter.

The house at Boskenna consists of a quadrangle erected at various periods, surrounding some older buildings. The whole, except the older buildings, is of dressed granite. The west wing, the north gable of which flanks the north door and the south gable of which is in a line with the south front, has apparently supplied a model for the rest of the building. It is two storeyed, with mullioned windows. A coat-of-arms carved in stone, Paynter impaling Pawlett, bearing the date 1678 is inserted in the south gable of the west wing. It was rebuilt at this time. The south front was renovated in 1858, and furnished with dormer windows. In 1886 the east wing was added.

9

Early owners before the Paynters came

In A SHORT HISTORY OF ST.BURYAN, Rev. C.B.Crofts wrote:

BOSKENNA (Boskene,1306) meaning doubtful, either "The House of Kenna"(most unlikely) or "The House on the Cliff". About 1400 was held by the Benne family, but passed into the hands of the Killigrews.

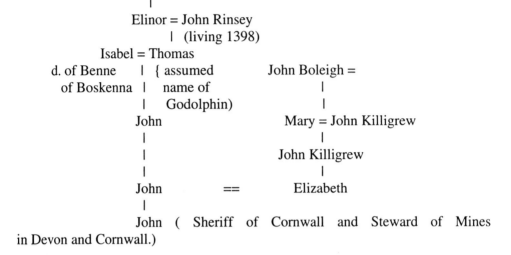

```
   William Godolphin =
                      |
              Elinor = John Rinsey
                  |   (living 1398)
        Isabel = Thomas
  d. of Benne  |  { assumed      John Boleigh =
  of Boskenna  |    name of                   |
               |    Godolphin)                |
            John                   Mary = John Killigrew
               |                           |
               |                      John Killigrew
               |                           |
            John          ==          Elizabeth
               |
            John  ( Sheriff of Cornwall and Steward of Mines
```
in Devon and Cornwall.)

Rev. Crofts in his 'EGLOSBERRIE' published in 1936 refers to the Church Screen which 'to judge by the two coats of arms carved on the beam, was the gift of Levelis of Trewoofe and Godolphins of Boskenna'.

In the 16th century the manor of Boskenna included lands in St.Buryan, Paul and other parishes. At that time it was held by the Godolphins. In the 15th century Thomas Godolphin married Isabel daughter of Benne of Boskenna, who was the great-grandfather of John Godolphin, Sheriff of Cornwall 1504.

Sir William Godolphin held lands in St.Buryan in the reign of Henry VIII and he, or his son Sir William, made settlements of Boskenna in 1536 and 1551. Sir William junior had two daughters coheirs, Margaret who married Sir Robert Dennys, and Grace who married Sir John Sydenham. In 1560 Boskenna was conveyed toWilliam Gilbert, Bernard Penrose, and John Tregian. In 1584 it was the residence of Walter Carthew, and for the next almost 100 years it was the property of the Carthews. Admiral Carthew was the last of the family there.

The Paynter's early ancestors

In the battle of Poictiers, France, 1356 Sir George Camborn, captain of the archers, the traditional ancestor of the Paynters of Boskenna, led the foremost rank. It was customary for a dismounted knight to lead the archers. Sir George was knighted on the field of battle and bore the crest 3 broken arrows.

Some generations later a descendant John de Camborn became an apprentice to a painter in London, training to be a highly skilled craftsman. He appears to have quarrelled with William Paynter of Gwinear, Cornwall, and killed him. John fled to Ireland, stayed a long time, then came to St.Erth, Cornwall, and set up a painter's shop. He took the name of William Camborn alias Paynter, married William Paynter's widow Elinor (nee Wilton) about 1558 and took over William's lands. He received a grant of arms from the Garter King of Arms 22 July 1569.They were living at Deverall, Gwinear and owned Trelissic Walbert at St.Erth. Elinor had seven children of the first marriage and one of the second.

Famous Paynters

There were some famous Paynters who were not in the direct line of the Boskenna Paynters. For instance, David Paynter senior, settled with some of his family at Dale in Pembrokeshire and later a descendant, another David acquired Dale Castle in 1669, and sold it again in 1699 to his son-in-law William Allen. The latter David became High Sheriff in 1743.

Another descendant Admiral James Aylmer Paynter was elected Mayor of Bath in 1874. Having met the Lord Mayor of London and his Lady, he invited them to visit him at Bath. The Lord Mayor, Mr. William James Richmond Cotton brought the glass coach and other State coaches, with his two Sheriffs and their wives, to Bath from Paddington. Great was the excitement as they proceeded through the streets in the glass coach on a sunny June day with 60,000 spectators lining the route.

Another very distant relative of the Boskenna Paynters on a different line was Rachel (Welsh name Rahel-o-Fon) 1845-1916, granddaughter of Joseph Cox Paynter a toll officer at Port Madoc. She started preaching with the Baptists at 20. It has been said, she was one of the greatest preachers Wales ever produced. She was invited on a preaching tour of the U.S.A. and when living in Ixonia joined the Calvinistic Methodists. While in Ohio she met and married Edward Davies a prosperous wagon maker. After her husband died she was ordained a minister at the age of 44 and carried on preaching all her life. Her son Joseph gave a 50ft. stained glass window to the Washington National Cathedral to her memory. Joseph became a lawyer and later Ambassador to Russia under Franklin D. Roosevelt. The President said to Joseph "You and I were most fortunate in the greatness of our mothers. She was one of the greatest women I have known".

Chapter 2

THE 1st FRANCIS PAYNTER OF BOSKENNA 1639 -1724

Trelissick, St Erth.

William Cambon alias Paynter, mentioned earlier, had a son George alias Paynter of Deverill. His son Arthur Paynter took over Trelissic St. Erth. Arthur and his descendants were lawyers and very much on the make. By industry and legal trickery they secured a fine estate. They would advance money on mortgage and then over a very long period the property would pass into their hands. No doubt Artur and his family lived well. In evidence before a Special Commission in 1598 it was stated that Arthur Paynter had 'a wayne load of Wyne from a captured ship'. When Arthur Paynter died in 1630 his son William inherited Trelissick. The property which dates back to 890 AD, had at one time been an abbey. It was by this time a large house with its own pier (where ore was loaded from Ennys Wheal Virgin mine nearby), and a tidal river flowed two miles upstream navigable by 50 ton vessels before Hayle Causeway was built. William collected money for the Royalist Cause, and was lucky not to lose his estates when they lost the Civil War.

Soon after his father died William Paynter commenced buying land at St. Buryan, and it was his son Francis who came from Trelissick to be the first Paynter of Boskenna (see Paynter Tree). In 1632 William married Jane Keigwin, and it was Jenkin Keigwin, great grandfather of Francis, who was killed by raiding Spaniards at Mousehole in 1595 defending his Keigwin home. Richard Keigwin, his son, was *'killed by Spanishers in 1636'*.

1st Francis Paynter at Boskenna, St.Buryan.

However, it is to Francis Paynter that I would draw your attention - born at Trelissick, St. Erth in 1639, a younger son of William and Jane. His brother, also William, became Rector of Exeter College, Oxford, and Vice-Chancellor of Oxford University. His elder brother, Arthur, married Mary Praed and lived at Trelissick, St. Erth, the family home. William Paynter, the elder, acquired Boskenna, St. Buryan, for his son Francis about 1676. Apparently the 1st Francis was already in residence at Boskenna, possibly from the time of his marriage in 1670. He was practising law and was sending out letters from there, and from 1672 the parish registers for St.Buryan record baptisms for the children. The property was purchased on a mortgage from a cousin, Admiral Carthew, who had gambled all his money away. Francis Paynter allowed him to remain at Boskenna, living in one room with his two dogs. Carthew became the huntsman in charge of the local pack of hounds of which he had previously been the owner. In Bottrell's LEGENDS AND

HEARTHSIDE STORIES there is one about his daughter Nellie who eloped with a pirate. She came back 20 years later on the day of her father's funeral very rich but too late to save Boskenna for her father (see Appendix).

In 1676, Francis Paynter bought Lower Boskennal, St. Buryan, from a Mr. Tippett and also purchased Higher Boskennal on a 99 year Lease and there he lived whilst improvements were being made at Boskenna. In later years he returned to this property and was known as Francis Paynter of Boskennal.
(In the name Boskennal, the last syllable is emphasised, in the name Boskenna, the middle syllable.)

TRELISSICK, ST. ERTH,. Birthplace of the 1st Francis Paynter

In Lake's Parochial History of Comwall it is recorded that "Mr. Francis Paynter by his skill and husbandry ... and some helps of the law, has purchased to himself a very fair younger brother's inheritance. Though this place (Boskenna) lies near the sea and very much exposed, yet has this gentleman by means of furze ricks and other ingenious contrivances raised several fair walks of trees about it, and made it a pleasant seat." To add to his comfort Francis had brought with him from Trelissick a great Jacobean

13

bed. Francis married twice. There were children by his first wife and one son James, survived. Francis's second wife was Margaret Pawlett, whom he married in 1670. She was the daughter of Sir Henry Pawlett of Kilburn Priory, Middlesex. She brought considerable property with her. Wealthy though she was, she allowed the servants only half an egg each for breakfast. In the St. Buryan parish register is recorded that the Dean of St. Buryan leased tithes for three years to Hugh Jones, Esq. of Penrose and to Francis Paynter of Boskenna amounting to £240 at 30th March, 1683.

Dubious transactions

Francis Paynter acquired wealth in various ways and not always honourably it would seem, sometimes in collusion with his brother Arthur of Trelissick. In 1665 one of Francis Paynter's cousins, a William Paynter of Tremearne, Germoe, had

debts, some of which Francis Paynter paid off for him. There were other debts and William assigned the rents and profits on two-thirds of Tremearne to Francis, who in return went bail for him. Later, William, equally as dishonourable, sold lands (which were already mortgaged to Francis) to a Christopher Cork. Francis seized possession of those lands in 1680 and *"kept more than his legal entitlement"*, so William said in court in 1681. Francis promised to secure William's release from Bodmin jail if he signed certain deeds over to him. This William did without reading them first hoping to be freed, but it is said, Francis left him in prison. When William was eventually set free his cousin Thomas Hawkins had him arrested again for a small debt. He was kept at the Bailiffs House for a few days, then taken as prisoner to Francis Paynter's house at St. Buryan. There Francis forced him to sign over property to him.

Conversely, Francis was considered a religious man. Books on Divinity were to be found in his library. His eminent brother, William Paynter D.D. (earlier referred to) became rector of Wootten, Northamptonshire. His own son, Thomas, was curate of Sennen and St. Levan, later vicar of Sithney. Francis had obvious church connections.

Penzance Town Clerk

By 1693 Francis had become Town Clerk of Penzance. Various references to him are recorded by the late Peter Pool in his 'History of Penzance" more especially in connection with the dispute between John Carveth and Thomas Rowe, Vicar of Madron. Carveth had served two terms as mayor.

After a disputed election there were two mayors of Penzance. Carveth attempted to appoint a new curate of St. Mary's Chapel without reference to the Vicar of Madron. The Vicar acted firmly, supported by the Bishop, Sir Jonathan

Trelawny. Francis Paynter took a letter to the bishop who was at that time in London. Carveth was forced to abandon both claims. Francis Paynter was appointed as one of the commissioners to swear in the new mayor.

No doubt an interesting meeting took place between Bishop Trelawney and Francis Paynter. The bishop was Dean of St. Buryan as well as Bishop of Exeter. (Bishop Trelawney, one of the six Bishops who had been imprisoned in the Tower, was an ancestor of the late Diana, Princess of Wales).

The Paynters were ardent Royalists and had melted down the family silver for the cause. For many years over the mantelpiece there hung an oil painting of James II. Beside it were two little medallions of Charles I and his queen Henrietta Maria, together with a chair that Charles I had sat on, which were among prized possessions. Another

BOOK WITH TWO SILVER CLASPS

historical memento was a book with silver clasps, containing a manuscript list of all the ships in the Navy in 1701. Eventually, Francis moved back to Boskennal and his son the 2nd Francis took possession of Boskenna.

Raiding Frenchmen

There was always a certain danger of isolated raids carried out from foreign vessels on those who lived near the shore. The story is told of what happened on 29th July 1711. A French privateer landed at St. Loy (Boskenna foreshore) robbed a house and afterwards went on shore (again) at Penberth, carried away two boats, some sheep and two men from the village and made them bring their women on board "ye boates". They forced the women to compound for their freedom and after the penalty was paid, kept the men and the tackle and sent the women and the boats to the shore ... This same Frenchman afterwards landed men and took some sheep at Porthgwarra, These kinds of incidents would no doubt have made going out of the family home a hazard for well-brought up young ladies, or anyone else, who lived near the coast.

The second Francis and his brother James, had a much younger sister Diana. Ustick writes in July, 1711, "Mr James Paynter is gone for Diana and Mr. Hawkins; the person she dined with at Burnewhall". It seems that Diana, aged seventeen, had gone off to her cousin's house and James was sent to bring her back. It was no time for allowing young ladies of seventeen too much liberty, however innocent the occasion. Even though it was not yet dark; dinner was an early meal and Burnewhall but a mile from Boskenna.

We have to look at the first Francis's life as being led in very harsh times and although many of his actions cannot be admired, he laid the foundations for the Paynter family at St. Buryan for many generations. Nine generations of the Paynter family lived at Boskenna over a period of two hundred and eighty years. Their stay is fascinating and their colourful lives are a part St.Buryan history.

Will of the First Francis Paynter of Boskenna and Boskennal 1723

PAYNTER, FRANCIS of Boskennal in Buryan, by his will 13 June 1723, proved in the Peculiar court of the Deanery of Burian Chapel Royal 1 Aug. 1724, gave to his wife Margaret Paynter, the tenements called Boskennal, which he purchased from Mr. Tippett, to hold during her life, also the tenements which he held by leases from Rt. Hon. Hugh Boscawen and John Trevanion to hold during her life, also the messuages called Galligan in Burian, and all the messuages and houses in Burian church town which he held by lease, during her life, and as long as she lives at Boskennal the use of all the furniture, etc. To his dear friend and son in law Francis Paynter of Trelissick, his son Francis Paynter of Boskenna, and his friends William Gwavas of Penzance, and George Veale of Trevailer, all his lands, &c. in Wilsdon and Acton in Middlesex upon trust. All his chattell leases, lands &c. called Rosemodress, Roselucomb, the Gawes, the Ninnicks and the Tregiffiens all in Burian, to them in trust, to sell, pay debts and equally divide to all his children living (except to his eldest son Francis Paynter on whom he settled an estate in his lifetime). All his other lands in Burian, Breag, Marazion, etc., which he settled on his son Francis on his marriage, if his heirs fail, then to his son Thomas Paynter, then in default to his son Arthur Paynter and so on to other sons; Overplus of sale to his daughter Mary, wife of Thomas Haweis of Chincoose, gent., her share to remain till T. Haweis settle a jointure of some estate on his wife. To the indigent of S. Burian £4, To the indigent of Sennen, St. Levan and St. Erth £2 each.

At the end he wrote: In witness my hand and seal 13 June 1723. Here I take of my seal and declare this to be my last will and testament, Fran. Paynter. Witnesses Mary Paynter, Stephen Bodinar and Francis Carne.

(Boskenna appears to have been mainly owned at this time by the Keigwins of Mousehole and purchased later by the 2nd Francis Paynter.)

Family of Francis 1

Francis had a son James by his first marriage. James proclaimed the Pretender, King James III, in the Market Place at St. Columb in 1714 on the day after Queen Anne died. He was sent to Newgate and tried for High Treason. He claimed to be a judge in Cornwall so was tried at Launceston, where he was acquitted by a packed Jacobite jury, and returned home in triumph, and was received with bonfires and celebrations. (Many would have preferred James to be king, rather than George of the House of Hanover). His second wife Margaret Pawlett bore him 13 children between 1672 and 1695, all baptised at St Buryan.(Burke's Landed Gentry confuses Francis I with his son-in-law Francis who was born in 1662. The latter would not be producing children at 10 years old!)

Details below of three of the children of the 1st Francis

1 His daughter Margaret married her first cousin Francis Paynter of Trelissick, St. Erth. He was one of the clerks of the Admiralty, and later General Receiver of Prize Money which was due to captors. Their daughter Mary married John Hearle of Penryn, and they had three daughters. The eldest, Harriet married Rev. Henry Hawkins Tremayne of Heligan, the second Jane married Francis Hearle Rodd of

BOSKENNAL, where 1st Francis Paynter retired. From left to right, my father, Vivian Hosking, James Henry Warwick and baby Leonard on horse with employee ?? Berriman and my grandfather, Augustus, on right.

Trebartha, and the youngest daughter married Capt. Samuel Wallis R.N. well known discoverer of Otaheite, now called Tahiti, one of the Society Islands in the Pacific about half way between Australia and Peru. (See 'tree' on page 1).

2 His daughter Mary, born 1682 , married Thomas Haweis of Redruth and had a son Thomas born 1709. They were ancestors of Mary Davies Haweis who married Reginald Paynter in 1858.

3 His son born 1676 became the 2nd Francis Paynter of Boskenna.

Chapter 3

THE SECOND FRANCIS PAYNTER 1676 - 1762.

The 2nd Francis Paynter of Boskenna was certainly a chip off the old block, and was very sharp in business. His father held Bosliven in Buryan on a lease, and in 1711 Usticke of Nancealverne tried to recover possession through a Mr. Davies of Cork, who was evidently a necessary party to the matter. Usticke did not know what he was up against. His diary 20 April 1711 reads:. *"I produced for Mr. Davies my title to Bosliven. He read the case but made no answer. The same day he took his leave."*

A week later Usticke sent Francis 2nd notice of his entry into Bosliven. Within 48 hours he received the rent, £2.10.0 and the next day:

"Mr. Francis Paynter junr. writt me by his brother James that he had not my letter until last night and never heard of Mr. Davies of Cork being in the country until he saw my letter, and then heard he was gone"

Usticke tried to get an interview with James Paynter. But having tracked him down to Trevethoe, the Praed home near Lelant, was told that he had gone out in a boat and that 'they had set nets for catching fish.' That does not sound very convincing! Francis and his father held on to Bosliven, and the farm was still on the Boskenna rent rolls in 1880.

Legal affairs

The 2nd Francis Paynter was admitted to the Court of Kings Bench at Launceston on 23 July 1730, and Solicitor of the Court of Chancery on 27 February 1730.

In the year 1743/44 a dispute arose between Dr. Sykes, Dean of St. Buryan and Dr. Borlase, Vicar of Madron over the latter's claim to the tithes on fish caught at Penberth, St. Buryan. Dr. Sykes asked Francis to intervene. He wrote, *"I have desired Mr. Paynter to wait on you; and I dare say, when you talk together, it will be easy to determine this point"*.......

It took 3 letters and threat of Court action to resolve the case.

Rumours and buried treasure

In 1745 there were rumours that the Young Pretender Charles Stuart was hiding at Boskenna, at a time when Cornwall was thought to be in imminent danger of invasion. Rev John Pearce wrote in "The Wesleys in Cornwall": 'The lower sort of people' publicly insulted Mr. Paynter, as he passed along the roads, and the tinners of Breage and Germoe threatened to march to Boskenna, search the house and blow out the Pretender's brains. No doubt the lower sort of people remembered that, in 1714 at St. Columb Major, his kinsman had proclaimed James as King on the death of Queen Anne. Mr Paynter, to clear himself, invited Walter Borlase to come and search his house, which Borlase and some other justices did. They found nothing amiss and were invited to dinner. Many of the Cornish Gentry had Jacobite leanings. In 1715 Sir Richard Vyvyan of Trelowarren had been imprisoned as a Jacobite in the Tower. In 1745 a Cornish invasion was planned, and in Penzance a search for arms was requested. There were ships near Morvah with Jacobite sympathisers on board. One engaged a British warship off the Lizard. Charles Stuart sailed up to Scotland and the ill-fated '45 uprising.

There had been a suggestion that Francis was concerned in the 1745 Rebellion. In 1747 he was ordered to appear before the Justices at Plymouth. Believing he was being called to answer serious charges, and stood to lose all he possessed, he decided to hide his silver and jewellery. He left the house on horseback taking a couple of mules. He returned within the hour, and believed he had not been seen, as, he thought, all the people there had gone to celebrate at St. Buryan. Was it the Feast? .He had been seen from an attic window by a maidservant who had stayed home because she was unwell.

Soon after he set out for Plymouth taking with him his factor, the only other person who knew where the treasure was hidden. He needed the factor to give evidence on his behalf.

When Francis, sweating with anxiety, came into the presence of the Justices, he was astounded to learn that he had been sent for to have an honour bestowed on him! Now the mystery -He seems to have disappeared for a long time. Some thought he died of cholera with his factor at Hayle. Some have tried to find his hidden treasure. However, 15 years later, more mystery his second will showed him as then living at Boskennal with his wife and, he is recorded as being buried at St. Buryan 21st March 1762 at the age of 85.

Will of Francis II of Boskennal buried 1762

His wife Mary inherited all his Somerset lands, all the property at Egloshayle. Boskenna 'which I purchased from James Keigwin,' Rosewall, Lefra and Tregadgwith in St Buryan. Trewey in St. Levan. Leasehold in Rosemodress (from Buller), all these for life and household goods etc. To children: Margaret Pender £100, her son Benjamin £10,. her other children: Mary, Francis, Margaret, and Peter Pender £100 each. To grandson Francis Paynter- Rosmodress and all tin bounds in St.Just and Breage.

In 1713 the 2nd. Francis had married a widow named Mary Hawkey from Colan. Said to be unpopular, a close, disagreeable woman, and yet Francis expresses his love for her in his will of 1730 and in his will proved 1762.

19

Three children grew to adulthood. Four died young. Mary married Samuel Thomas of Tregellis.

Margaret married Bejamin Pender of Budock Vean, Penryn, and had 8 children. Two died of smallpox in 1756. The Penders were formerly of Trevider, St. Buryan. The 3rd Francis, of whom more later.

Mary Hawkey was the widow of Thomas Hawkey who had a legal practice in St.Colomb. She married the 2nd Francis Paynter, and their son Francis III may have carried on the firm for a short while, but it was the latter's second son, Francis the Wit, younger brother of James, with whom we associate the firm Paynter and Whitford, solicitors.

Chapter 4

THE 3rd FRANCIS PAYNTER. 1716 - 1775

The 3rd Francis wasted much of the family fortune. If the first two were on the make the third struck the balance in no uncertain manner. *"What he did"* Mary Paynter wrote, *"I have not been able to discover with certainty, but it is said, he mortgaged the estate to a great extent, and so injured the property, that it took many years of careful management to bring it round."* Tom Paynter writes, *"One at least feels that Francis had some fun with his father's money, the brilliant end to the dark ages of the family."*

A painting of Francis may be still in existence. It shows him holding a book. He is wearing a white cravat and heavy lapelled waistcoat of oyster coloured silk, and I read that it is beautifully painted. My great grandmother Mary Ann Care said that in the time of Thomas Paynter it was hung in the attic facing the wall. Thomas did this to show his displeasure at what his grandfather had done to waste the family fortune. When Francis III died there was just about enough to pay for his funeral.

He became Registrar of the Court of the Peculiar of St. Buryan in 1744.

Threat to John Wesley.

When John Wesley was preaching from the hepping stock (stone steps) outside the church at St Buryan in 1766 Francis III appears to have threatened him with a whip.

FROM JOHN WESLEY'S DIARY.

Sunday 7 September 1766

"At eight I preached at Mousehole. Thence to Buryan Church: and as soon as the service was ended, preached near the Churchyard to a numerous congregation. Just after I began I saw a gentleman before me, shaking his whip, and vehemently to say something, but he was abundantly too warm to say anything intelligibly, so after walking awhile to-and-fro, he wisely took his horse and rode away."

Since Revd. Robert Corker was dead, Wesley could attend the Church service without fear of being insulted by him. Tradition has it that he used the mounting block as a pulpit. Who was the irate gentleman? Probably Francis III.

EXTRACT FROM THE ST. JUST WESLEYAN METHODIST
CIRCUIT MESSENGER   APRIL 1892

In connection with the incident at St Buryan above alluded to, one of our oldest members at Crowsanwray (a branch Society of Buryan), Mr Humphry Wallis tells how that his great grandfather, Mr. John Wallis of Crella Farm was present on that occasion. John, through duties, was unable to attend the ordinary morning service at the church, but came up in order to hear Mr. Wesley afterwards. The gentleman Mr. Wesley speaks of as "shaking his whip and vehemently striving to say something," Francis Paynter by name, as he came out of the church saw John quietly sitting on the old stone cross waiting for Mr,Wesley. Coming up to him, the squire, shaking his fist in his face, said, " Ah, John, you scoundrel, you couldn't come to the proper service, but you can come up to listen

to that rogue Wesley."

. Wesley had previously made a pro-Jacobite speech, and Francis did not want the people stirred up again. His father had been accused of harbouring the Pretender, threatened by miners, had his house searched, and later had been summoned to Plymouth for what as he thought at the time were pro-Jacobite activities.

The 3rd Francis was a churchwarden at St.Buryan in later life.

JOHN WESLEY (Rev Tom Shaw) threatened with a whip in 1766 by FRANCIS PAYNTER (the author) at St. Buryan

Mary Gully

Francis III was baptised at St Columb in 1716, and in 1740 married Mary Gully daughter of Samuel Gully of Gynhosken, near Tresillian about 5 miles from St. Columb .It has been said that her brother, in a violent temper, once threw a knife at a servant which unfortunately killed him. The matter was hushed up, but, it was said, Mary suffered so much from temper on her side of the family that she hesitated long before entering into the Paynter family who had a similar reputation.

Mary Gully used to collect her rents once a year from her tenants on her property near Wadebridge, always staying the night at Trekenning the home of her Paynter cousins. She was a very dignified lady, and the boys there enjoyed playing practical jokes. On one occasion they dyed her horses black, and blacked the coachman's face .She never found out until she was well on her way home, She spoke to the coachman and he turned round. The old lady was so angry she vowed she would never enter Trekenning again, and she never did.

Children of Francis III (see Family 'tree' of Paynters Part 2)
James- married Betty Wethered.

Francis- (the Wit) married Margaret Pender, (see below).

William- a lieutenant in the Navy and died young.

Charles- a lawyer in Penzance, married a Tucklift of Tyesh, and father of Edward and Frank, more later.

Henry- died unmarried

Harriet was lame, married Rev Owen Morris, minister Octagon Independent Chapel, South Parade, Penzance in 1798. No issue.

Frances, and three others died in infancy.

REAR APPROACH OF BOSKENNA HOUSE

Francis the Wit
Francis (see above), known as Francis the Wit, became a lawyer at St. Columb, and then head of the legal firm of what later became Paynter and Whitford. He was living at Trekenning in 1799 and died there in 1814. The firm had a number of influential clients- the Hearles of Penryn, the Lemons, Rodds, and Tremaynes. They also acted for the Williams of Carnanton, and as they came into the 19th

century Thomas Whitford became junior partner. Members of the Whitford family continue to be heads of the firm almost until the present day. Francis was distinguished for his wit and humour. He wrote a poem 'THE CONSULTATION', published in 1771, ridiculing the Dean of St. Buryan Hon. Nicholas Boscawen, youngest son of the first Viscount Falmouth, and so lost a valuable stewardship the Boscawens were going to give him. He infers in this libellous poem that Boscawen and his associates were a greedy and immoral crowd

.... a zealous priest
With avarice galled the groaning west;
Rapacious soul he seemed designed
By nature to oppress mankind:
His features, maugre all his art,
Disclosed the baseness of his heart;
For Satanus took care to place
A stamp upon his swarthy face ....
and another short extract:
1
Let commanders run mad,
For cold iron and lead,
And dream of great conquests and plunder
A bullet or thrust
Lays a hero in dust,
And all his rare schemes the turf under.
2
The learned physician,
Who kills by permission,
And hastens his patient's demise on,
Let him reckon his gains,
There's a corpse for his pains,
And a fee for prescriptions to poison.
3
Let the priest by o'erreaching,
By canting and preaching,
Endeavour to make his tithes double,
Unassisted by law
All the parson can do,
Is no better by G. than a bubble.

4

But in term or vacation,
How blest is the station,
Of lawyer in city or village
With clients attendant
Complainant defendant,
.Poor mortals devoted to pillage.

5

As bees pilfer honey,
So he plunders money,
And stuffs from all quarters his pocket
In short sir the law
Is the best trade I know
And he that says nay is a blockhead .

Algiers incident

In 1815 the Dey of Algiers imprisoned the British Consul.

John Pender Paynter, the fourth son of Francis the Wit was then Flag Lieutenant to Lord Exmouth, who sent him ashore to demand the Consul's release. The Dey seized John and put him in 'the Black Hole'. The city was successfully bombarded by the British Fleet 'for continued piracy'. John must have been very frightened, but he survived the Black Hole and the bombardment, and was promoted Commander. (Lord Exmouth as Edward Pellew spent some of his childhood at Hawkes Farm, Penzance.)

Ghost of lady in white

Tradition has it there was a daughter of Francis III named Ann. She was in disgrace because of her attachment to one beneath her station. A well on St. Loy cliff used to be called Miss Ann's Well, because she would sit there for hours watching the ships go by. Her sweetheart had been press ganged. She died young and broken hearted. On her death, it was said, the old nurse cursed the family saying, *"There will never be another daughter born here"*. Certainly there were none born for the next three generations. Apparently Ann's ghost appears to this day, dressed in white, walking along the avenue.

If you do not believe my tale try taking a horse and carriage around to the front of Boskenna House. They will appear to be terrified, and. that is why the drive was changed, now leading to the back of the house, when formerly it lead to the front!

Ghost of the 'Rocker'

If you are afraid of ghosts keep out of the woods at night, for there is said to be another apparition roaming around of a very strong man who resents trespassers there. He comes silently up behind you, and grips you suddenly with a hand on each arm, just above the elbow, lifts you up and shakes you till your bones and teeth rattle.

Cannon fire

A story was told by Great-grandmother Mary Ann Care about the Paynters of long ago. It was recorded by the late J. H. Care. It appears that a Paynter boy and his friend were on holiday from boarding school. Down among the trees at Boskenna was a spot called Ivy Castle where a cannon was placed, For a lark these boys fired it pointing it out to sea, and it hit a fishing boat killing the crew. The two lads were swiftly sent back to school and things went quiet. Many years later Boskennal Farm was up for letting. Several local farmers tried to secure it, but it was let to a farmer from the Midlands called Mr Brown. Time passed by and Mr. Brown died. On the day of the funeral when the people arrived at St. Buryan Churchyard the people saw that the Paynter vault was open, and then Mr. Brown, as they thought, was buried in it. The mystery was solved - it was the Paynter lad who fired the cannon from the cliff.

Chapter 5

JAMES PAYNTER `1748 - 1800

In his book Mr Tom Paynter enlightens us with the following:- In 1775 James, eldest son of Francis Paynter of Boskenna, took over the reins from his genial but dissolute father. He seems to have been a serious sort of man, which was, perhaps just as well for the property. Bosliven and Boskennal passed direct to James from his grandfather, who may have hoped that some of the property would thus survive.

James was very different from his predecessors. A kindly caring man, perhaps lonely too, and burdened with a shortage of cash to run the estate, which may also have affected his love life. It seems that for a long time he tried to win the hand of Miss Mary Beard elder daughter of Jonah Milford of Truro, but his proposals were not accepted.

Soon after Rev and Mrs Winter came from London on a visit to Boskenna bringing a young lady, Miss Betty Wethered with them. James, in 1787 at the age of 39, fell in love and married Betty daughter of Sarah Wethered of Clegg Hall, Lancashire. On her he made a marriage settlement of £200 a year for life.

In the early 1800s there was a tidal wave of conversion to Methodism in St Buryan as in the rest of Cornwall. Later a new Methodist Chapel was built in the village because the old one could not hold the people. At Boskenna the Calvinist Movement became very active. The Calvinists were an evangelical offshoot of the Church of England. They built their own Chapels and these were known as the Countess of Huntingdon's connection. The countess was converted by George Whitfield, considered by many as the greatest evangelical preacher of his day. The Countess of Huntington's Connection eventually joined the Congregationalists.

James and Betty Paynter were very united, and inspired by the Calvinist Movement. At Boskenna, the Hall (a long low room with a fine mullion window) was thrown open for religious services whenever they could get a preacher to stay in the house. Boase writes: 'The Pidwell family of Penzance, the Beard family of Paul and the Paynters between them supported a minister who went from one establishment to the other and probably also officiated at times in Penzance.'

The Chapel at Boskenna, now the entrance hall, was at various periods used by Mr. Henry Thornton, a rich philanthropist, the Rev Thomas Wills and others.

Rev Tom Shaw tells me that Rev Wills became curate at St. Agnes until 1778, after which he travelled for the Countess of Huntingdon, whose niece he had married. He went around preaching, drawing large crowds as a leader of the movement.

James Paynter must have been a long-suffering man. His wife had been, before her marriage, a companion to Mrs Selena Wills. The two ladies could not live apart, so the Rev. and Mrs. Wills came to live at Boskenna. Rev. Wills died in 1802 and there was a monument to him in St. Buryan Church. His wife Selena Wills stayed on another twelve years and was buried with him in St. Buryan Churchyard. She was the daughter of Rev. Grenville Wheler and Right Hon. Lady Catherine Wheler.

James' mother in law came to stay and was buried in St Buryan in 1792.

Ann Marriot of Rochdale, a relation of James died at Boskenna in 1810.

James as we have seen was very hospitable. He was glad to welcome his nephews and nieces at all times. He was also very patient, which was just as well, for in his later years he became partially paralysed and such an invalid that when he attended the bench of magistrates at Penzance, (which he did for many years almost to the end of his life), his footmen used to carry him into court.

James died in 1800. In his will he leaves *To Betty my beloved wife* £100 to be paid to her within six months of my death". He left all his Buryan property and Trewey land to John his elder son. To his younger son Thomas he left all his lands in Egloshayle. He also remembered his brothers Francis, Henry, Charles, and sister Harriet.

Mrs. Betty Paynter, wife of James.

Betty Paynter was conscientious and kind. Her diary showed she was very concerned about her spiritual life

She was famous in the neighbourhood for making medicines from herbs. In an old stone hut in the rockery she distilled her medicine. She compiled a large book of recipes. She carried out pickling preserving and cooking.

There were two life size portraits in the house showing her in a white-frilled cap and cambric fichu folded across her black satin dress.

FAMILY 'TREE' of PAYNTERS of BOSKENNA Part 2

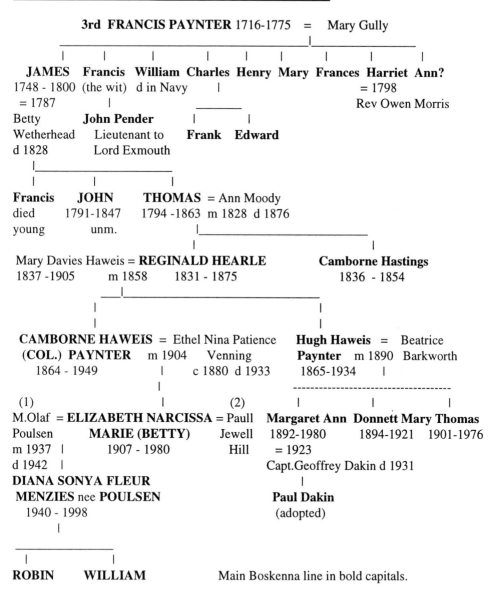

3rd FRANCIS PAYNTER 1716-1775 = Mary Gully

JAMES   Francis   **William**   Charles   Henry   Mary   Frances   Harriet   Ann?
1748 - 1800 (the wit)   d in Navy   = 1798
= 1787   Rev Owen Morris

Betty   **John Pender**
Wetherhead   Lieutenant to   **Frank   Edward**
d 1828   Lord Exmouth

Francis   JOHN   THOMAS = Ann Moody
died   1791-1847   1794 -1863 m 1828 d 1876
young   unm.

Mary Davies Haweis = **REGINALD HEARLE**   **Camborne Hastings**
1837 -1905   m 1858   1831 - 1875   1836 - 1854

CAMBORNE HAWEIS = Ethel Nina Patience   **Hugh Haweis** = Beatrice
  (COL.) PAYNTER   m 1904   Venning   **Paynter** m 1890 Barkworth
    1864 - 1949 | c 1880 d 1933   1865-1934 |

(1)   (2)   **Margaret   Ann   Donnett   Mary   Thomas**
M.Olaf = **ELIZABETH NARCISSA** = Paull   1892-1980   1894-1921   1901-1976
Poulsen   **MARIE (BETTY)**   Jewell   = 1923
m 1937 | 1907 - 1980   Hill
d 1942 | Capt.Geoffrey Dakin d 1931
DIANA SONYA FLEUR
 MENZIES nee **POULSEN**   **Paul Dakin**
   1940 - 1998   (adopted)

ROBIN   WILLIAM   Main Boskenna line in bold capitals.

Chapter 6

JOHN PAYNTER 1790 - 1847.

John, second son of James Paynter and Betty Wethered, grew up to a life of marked contrast to that of his earlier ancestors. When he was nearly ten his father died and he became owner of Boskenna, and for the next 28 years, apart from schooling, he lived there with his mother. She being morbidly conscientious, a dedicated Calvinist though kindly, and with a minister there and a chapel, he grew up to be a serious and lonely man. Even while he was at college she wrote long letters finishing up with religious advice and prayers. (She sent up to him also snipe woodcock, cakes, etc.)

He became a Magistrate, much respected, very learned, and much engrossed in his books.

It has been written that - "John Paynter will long be remembered in the West Country as a liberal landlord and kind neighbour; and for being more learned in the law than country justices usually are. It was a common saying in the West that 'the Squire of Boskenna knew more law than all the lawyers of Penzance put together!" He never married. He was very interested in agriculture, wrote many articles including one on growing early potatoes on the cliff. Another was on the employment of gas water as manure, written for the Royal Agriculture Society of England in 1840.

A painting of John Paynter by John Opie was sold at Boskenna in 1957.

Boskenna Home Farm

John Paynter let Boskenna Home Farm sometime about 1820 to William Jelbart and his wife Elizabeth nee Jacka my gt. gt. gt. grandparents, and their descendants the Cares and the Hoskings remained tenants of the Paynter family until 1957 when the estate was sold.

In 1820 the farmhouse of Boskenna Home Farm was attached to the mansion, but a few years later, possibly about 1850, the present farmhouse was built.

Electrifying

The following is contained in "A HISTORY OF WEST CORNWALL HOSPITAL, PENZANCE". In 1821 "John Paynter Esq. of Boskenna has this day presented to the dispensary an Electrifying Machine for the use of the dispensary patients and to be forever the property of the institution. Mr. Paynter has also assented to the proposal made by Dr. Forbes that the said machine can be used by private patients". The above statement is interesting and may be regarded as the early foundation of the present Physiotherapy Department of the hospital.

Also, in 1826 the Hospital were trying to buy land at North Parade, Penzance from John's cousin Mr. Francis Paynter for a dispensary, but nothing came of it.

Edward Paynter and Sir Rose Price

In 1824 John's cousin Edward was prosecuted by Sir Rose Price of Trengwainton for killing 5 partridges at Bosliven, for a dinner party at Boskenna, at which dinner party Sir Rose Price was a guest. They were John's partridges, shot on John's land, for John's dinner party. Edward had a shooting licence but it was not valid in Cornwall.

For 8 years John had allowed Sir Rose to bring his hounds over Bosliven land, and he would be doing so the following day.

I have a personal interest in this story for the tenant of Bosliven was John Eddy my 3x great uncle. John Eddy actually delivered the game to Boskenna. Sir Rose tried to trap him into giving evidence against his landlord, and made him and Edward and John Paynter appear before a jury at Launceston Assizes rather than Penzance where feelings ran high.

The following is a very brief extract from defence summing up, *"Gentlemen, you have learned from that respectable farmer (John Eddy), that Sir Rose Price had received from Mr Paynter himself, year after year, the privilege of shooting over his entire property, without any restraint of any kind. .... This is a Baronet! A man of condition in this county ; he has actually come hither to bring before you Mr. Edward Paynter, for the purpose of extracting from his purse several penalties under the game laws, because this young gentleman, in compliance with the request of his own cousin, courteously went out to procure that sort of luxury for the table at which Sir Rose Price was to be a guest a few days later.*

Edward was fined a nominal £5 at a time when game laws were very harsh.

This was not the only time Sir Rose's passion for Game Laws got him into trouble. He was a controversial figure, but is well remembered. When invasion by the French seemed imminent he trained companies of infantrymen to protect West Cornwall. He was a founder member of the Morrab Gardens Library, widened roads, and built Jamaica Terrace and Jamaica Place, Heamoor, for his employees. Why Jamaica? Sir Rose Price owned sugar plantations in Jamaica with slaves. He also employed workers from West Cornwall out there as clerks, sugar mill managers etc.

Woodcocks and felspar

From *"A Guide to the Mounts Bay and the Lands End 1828"*.

Boskenna, the seat of John Paynter, Esq., a highly romantic spot, abounding with woodcocks, and, which under the direction of a skilful landscape gardener might be made emulate in beauty any of the charming villas that adorn the undercliff of the Isle of Wight.

On this estate there is a superficial quarry of decomposing granite which the mineralogist ought to visit for the purpose of obtaining some remarkable fine specimens of felspar in separate crystals, which may be easily removed from the mass in which they embedded.

Woodcocks seemed to have been very numerous in the early 1800s!

Loans

There is a mortgage 1845 showing that John Paynter lent James Bosustow £552 on Clapper Mill, near Lamorna. occupied by James Permewen and Sampson Hosking

John allowed a cousin Frank Paynter, brother of Edward, to manage his property for him which was very unfortunate, for Frank defrauded the estate, and also borrowed £1000 from John who had agreed to be bound over for him. (Note for Historians: Frank built Clarence House in Penzance).

John's mother dies

In 1828 John's mother Betty died without having any previous illness. She was 79. One morning the maid entered her room with hot water, found her and ran to call Mrs Jelbert at the Home Farm, grandmother to Mary Ann Care, my great grandmother. At that time the farm house was joined to Boskenna House. John and the servants did all they could but it proved a fatal seizure. A servant described the scene, *"John stood by the bed, and in a voice shaken with emotion said,' What shall I do? Mother is dying and it's Tom's wedding day!"* It was indeed the wedding day of his brother to Ann Moody in Somerset.

There was no way they could get down to Boskenna in time to see his mother. The couple were married, and came down as soon as the news reached them. It was a sad honeymoon.

Alone

While John's mother was alive he regularly took her visiting neighbours, and friends came to the house, but when she died his world fell apart. He continued writing articles on agriculture, but stopped visiting his friends. They got tired of him not returning their calls, and no longer came to Boskenna. He continued with his work as magistrate but his life became increasingly lonely. He became so engrossed in his books that he was not bothering with his meals, and half starved himself.

A few years before he died he signed a lease whereby for a peppercorn rent to trustees he became tenant of Boskenna in his lifetime, and so avoided death duties for his brother Thomas.

Omen

An interesting tale is told of the impending death of John Paynter.

Mary Ann (later Mrs. Care) and one of her servant girls were milking cows out in the field as they often did in the summertime. As they milked, both saw eight magpies walking up the field towards them in four pairs, just like a set of bearers at a funeral. Mary Ann instinctively had a premonition of death.

On the evening of New Year's Day 1847 as was his wont, John entertained 30 of his poorer neighbours and his servants to a party. He was alone in his study longer than usual and when the servants went to inform him of the departure of his guests they found him lying on the hearth rug having a seizure. The doctor was sent for and got him to bed but he died within a few hours.

His funeral was described by old Mrs. Berryman of Lamorna as *"The grandest sight I ever saw - the first time I ever saw a hearse - I didn't know what it was. To see the carriages and the yards and yards of black cloth - the gentry came from miles around - strings of carriages and people following them, reaching all the way from Boskenna Gate to Buryan Churchtown .... I never seen such a sight, except perhaps when Augustus Smith was buried"*.

Chapter 7

THOMAS PAYNTER 1794 - 1863, brother of John.

Thomas succeeded his brother John as owner of Boskenna in 1847.

He was only six when his father died, and grew up to be a man with a great sense of public duty.

He was educated at Tiverton School, and then at Trinity College, Cambridge where he got his B.A. in 1816 and M.A. in 1824. He became Barrister-at-Law in 1823.

He married in 1828 Ann Moody only daughter of Aaron Moody of Kingsdon, Somerset. She, like his mother, was a deeply religious woman. She cared much for her family but did not show tenderness to them. Her dress was plain without jewellery.

After working for a while as Revising Barrister for Suffolk and Norfolk from 1833 he came back to Cornwall as Recorder of Falmouth, Helston, and Penzance.

Lamorna Quarry

Thomas worked hard to help restore the family fortune. he was so disgusted that his grandfather had wasted so much of the Paynter inheritance that he had his grandfather's portrait consigned to the attic facing the wall. Mrs. Mary Paynter, Colonel's mother, in the 1890s wrote that Thomas leased Lamorna Quarry on the west side of the cove to Capt Owen, a close friend, who paid six pence a ton for the granite. She believed that together they had the pier built, and put up a crane. This was to lift the quarried stone into ships, which was then transported to London for building the Thames Embankment and other works..

She also believed that Thomas and Capt Owen also had a Quarry manager's house built, Cliff House, with a bell tower, and a large room for a mission church built for the quarry workers. (Capt. Owen was a very religious man). The quality of the granite on the west side was very poor, and eventually Capt Owen became bankrupt. Cliff House was later much enlarged and is now the Lamorna Cove Hotel.

Mrs Powell of Trewoofe believes that Cliff House was built at the instigation of the Freemans of Penryn. They had the lease from Lord Falmouth of the quarry on the east side of the cove, and this quarry was started in 1853.

Later Thomas Paynter's widow (Ann Paynter nee Moody) made a large contribution to the expense of the new mission chapel at Lamorna. This later became a Sunday School and then a day school. Now it is a village hall. She also provided a harmonium for St.Buryan Church.

St. Buryan School

Thomas after much time, trouble, and correspondence got the village school (now the Village Hall) transferred from the Charity Commission to the Elementary Schools. He also provided a playing field for the girls behind the school. His efforts were crowned with success, for within a few years there were 190 pupils registered at that school.

A list of the Trustees of the School in 1847 reads:- Messrs. Thomas Paynter and Reginald Paynter (aged 16), Boskenna; Rev. John Tonkin, Lelant; John Permewan, Trelew; James Permewan, Tregadgwith; Robert Harvey, Pendrea; John Mitchell, Borah; John Wallis, Trevorgans; John Saundrey, Bosfranken; Charles Jacka, Selina; Wm. Tregear, Trevore; James Tonkin, Boskennal; Rd. Hodge Esq., Truro.

(History repeats itself for in 1996 after much time effort and correspondence, those concerned have got St Buryan Primary School 'opted out', an independent school, which, with excellent teachers and modern facilities is going from strength to strength).

London Magistrate

From 1841 to 1863 he was a magistrate in London, first in Hammersmith and Wandsworth Police Court, and then in Westminster Police Court.

He wrote a pamphlet, The Practice at Elections, being plain instructions for the guidance of Sheriffs and other returning officers and their poll clerks.... by Thomas Paynter, Esq. Barrister-at-Law. He also had printed for private circulation, *Considerations on the office and duties of a Metropolitan Police Magistrate.*

Restoring Boskenna

Thomas was very determined to restore the family fortune and Boskenna to its former glory. When he came into the estate in 1847 he was living in London, and allowed the Rev. Farr, curate of St. Buryan, to live in the house for five years.

On the south wall of the house is a carving *Restored 1858*

He also invited farmers from Lincolnshire to become tenants of some of his farms, to raise the standard of farming in St. Buryan. Two of them were James Webster at Boskennal (148 acres), and Thomas Patch at Trewoofe (99 acres). They all wore red waistcoats!

Thomas lived very carefully, no luxuries, and set about restoring Boskenna in conjunction with Judge Charles Dacres Bevan, a close friend, to whom he had leased the house for 20 years. While Bevan had the lease it did not bar the Paynter family living or staying there for short periods. Bevan was constantly lending the house to Thomas Paynter, and often gave half crowns and shillings to his poorer neighbours.

Mary Davis Paynter, Reginald's wife wrote, *"When I came as a young bride in 1858 driving all the way from Plymouth to Penzance in a coach, the avenue was the chief entrance, though there was never a lodge".*

35

The old approach made a sweep and brought the visitor to the seaward side of the house. Judge Bevan took the drive straight to the back door. It was the shorter route but that was not all. It was noticed that the horses often got out of hand where the avenue crossed the track leading from the house to the sea, especially at night, and on one dark evening they shied and bolted. There was an accident, and a change seemed prudent, (ghostly stories abounding in the area).

St Buryan Artillery Corps

In about 1850 Justice Bevan started a volunteer Artillery Corps at St Buryan which consisted at the time of about 40 men. (Presumably this is why the village Drill Hall was built). Bevan took a great interest in the Battery, and had a gun mounted on Carn Boscawen where he trained men to fire at a barrel out at sea. Later he would invite the men to supper.

An Artillery Band was formed. (An Independent Brass Band was also started, and this later became the Buryan Brass Band).

In 1883 it was called the Duke of Cornwall's Artillery Volunteers (7th Battery) (Lieut. John Nicholls, commanding.)

By 1913 this Territorial unit was called 51st Cornwall (Duke of Cornwall's) Medium Brigade Royal Garrison Artillery (Left Section, No2 Heavy Battery); Lt.Col. Francis F.Oats T.D. commanding. Gerald Male tells me it was disbanded in 1914 when War broke out. Among those who had been in it at that time were H. Payne, J.T.Warren, J. Mitchell, C.T.Lugg, and C.T.Johns.

The Paynters continued to own the Drill Hall up to the late 1930s.

Camborne Hastings Paynter

Thomas suffered a great loss when his younger and favourite son died.
Camborne Hastings Paynter, born 1836, was Ensign in the 26th regiment Cameronians. He went out with his men to assist at the Great Fire at Newcastle on Tyne on the 6th Oct. 1854, and was killed as the result of an explosion when a wall fell on him. He was only 18, and his Bible lay open as he left to go on duty.

Death of Thomas Paynter

For many years Thomas suffered greatly with eczema. Having a fiery temper and an iron will he must have been difficult to live with, but his wife nursed him patiently and did her best to make him happy. His daughter-in-law recorded the following:- *"My recollection of Thomas Paynter is of a tall thin old man with white hair, and a fresh colour in his face, of a stern and irritable temperament. His own sons stood in awe of him, but he was kindly to me as a young bride.*

He died in Thurloe Square, London. I recollect well the night when we were all called up to see him for the last time. His wife, Reginald his eldest son, and I his daughter-in-law.

He lay in the dining room on a small iron bedstead that he used latterly, and seemed in no pain. He motioned me to him and wanted to say something, but he could not speak intelligibly. Poor man! How often I wish he could have seen his two grandsons for I know it was a bitter disappointment to him to die without any prospect of an heir to the Boskenna estate".

His Will 1862

The Will of Thomas, dated 13 May 1862, contained almost 11,500 words, (over one third of this book), and was very complicated, so involved that not even the lawyers could understand it. He left property in trust for his wife and son Reginald entailed for Reginald's eldest son (yet unborn) and then to younger sons and daughters. If Reginald had no family a distant cousin Joshua Paynter or his family were to be the eventual heirs.

The Will included the following lines:- The inheritor to bear the Arms of Camborne quarterly and to use the name Camborne in addition to or in place of surname.

(General Joshua Paynter was appointed Inspector of Military Hospitals in 1867 after serving through the Crimea War. He had the difficult task of reorganising the medical services).

Will of Ann Paynter widow of Thomas 1875

In her will proved 6 Feb. 1877 Ann directed that such of the furniture, plate, books, pictures, china etc. as were possessed by her, be left in trust for whichever of her grandsons Camborne Haweis Paynter or Hugh Haweis Paynter should have Boskenna.

What is so amazing is that she left the residue to Edward Paynter a second cousin of her husband Thomas with legacies to Edward's brothers, the servants, and others, and nothing more to her grandsons, and yet it was Edward's father Frank who had borrowed £1000 and defrauded the Boskenna estate a few years earlier!

The Will was found to be valid when tested in the Probate court.

Bible presented to employee

Miss Ann Wright has a Family Bible with the inscription *'Bible presented to Nanny Hocking who had worked at Boskenna as a cook until she left to be married (March 16 1869).*
With Mrs. (?) Paynter's best wishes for her present and future welfare. Also presented to her were six Liverpool porcelain plates of Queen's Ware inscribed by Mrs Paynter.

This is the first named employee that I have found of Paynter staff at Boskenna. Unfortunately Nanny Hocking, who married an Oates of Tregeseal, St. Just, died at the birth of her second child in 1871.

Chapter 8

REGINALD HEARLE PAYNTER 1831 - 1875 and MARY 1837 - 1905

Engagement

Thomas had written to Mary Haweis on 30.Sept. 1857:-

My dear Miss Haweis.

I can scarcely express too strongly my gratification at my son having made a choice, than which he could not have made one more acceptable to me, or more calculated to secure his own happiness: it has, I assure you, raised him highly in my good opinion, and I do rejoice at your having consented to become a member of our family . I only wish, for your sake, that we were a more numerous and cheerful party to greet you, but you have already so increased our happiness, that your kindly influence will, I doubt not, render our home more joyful than it has long been; to you it should scarcely seem a strange one for from former alliances, your name is with us a household word, to say nothing of your father being one of my dearest and most valuable friends, which I am much pleased to see that your brother is becoming to Reginald, on whom his engagement will, I am persuaded , have a most beneficial effect.

Some months ago I reluctantly consented to lay out some money on Boskenna, to save it from ruin, and render it a more comfortable residence. I did so most unwillingly, but now that I may look forward to its becoming a habitation for you and Reginald I am rejoiced to have taken this step.

I trust that long years of happiness and usefulness await you there, and that your example will restore the memory of some of your predecessors still held in honourable remembrance.

Believe me, my dear Miss Haweis,
faithfully and affectionately yours
Thomas Paynter.

Reginald

Reginald married Mary Davies Haweis on the 8th Dec. 1858 at Hove, Brighton. Mary wrote of her husband: Reginald was an able man, good at mathematics and languages, was in the Army a few years, afterwards worked in the Civil Service, Deans Yard, Westminster, under Sir Edward Ryan, an intimate friend of his father's. He was a splendid swimmer and could ride well, travelled a good deal over Europe, and kept copious diaries. These were never found.

His name appears as Second Lieutenant in the 1853 Army List only. He was a member of the Junior Athenaeum Club. He was in lodgings, and died at

25 Limerston St. Chelsea, in 1875 at the age of 43, and was buried at Brompton Cemetery. He never left a will, and in the estate, proved in 1895, Mary received the princely sum of £61!

Reginald never held the Boskenna estate as he died while his mother was still in possession.

How little we know about Reginald! He poses many questions.

Why did Thomas say Mary's brother would have a beneficial effect on Reginald?

Why was so little recorded of Reginald's Army career?

Why did Mary not mention his relationship with her and the children?

Why was he in lodgings?

Why did he leave only about £61

Why was the estate proved 20 years late?

There may be a simple explanation.

Mary Davies Paynter, nee Haweis

Mary Davies Haweis was a distant cousin of her husband Reginald. His early ancestors were Jane or Joan Haweis, who died 1619, and Arthur Paynter of Trelissick, St. Erth. Three more times a Paynter married a Haweis. They are:-

1677 Jane Paynter of Trelissic m. Thomas Haweis of Kea.

1721 Mary Paynter of Boskenna m. Thomas Haweis of Redruth.

and of course 1858 Reginald Paynter m. Mary Davies Haweis

Mary's grandfather Dr. Thomas Haweis Rector of Aldwinkle, Northampton was a founder of the Church Missionary Society. He married three times before he had any children.

Mary's father Rev. John Oliver Willyams Haweis, was Rector of Slaugham, Sussex. He was loved by all who knew him. When he preached at Buryan he aroused such enthusiasm that the villagers took the horses out of the carriage and drew him themselves all the way back to Boskenna.

Ameer

Reginald's mother-in-law, Mary wife of the above Rev.J.O.W.Haweis, appears to have been the daughter of Thomas Davies, who served with the 76th Regiment of Foot in India and Ameer, an Indian lady of consequence and refinement. She stayed in India and in his will he gave a life interest in a large part of his estate 'to Ameer in Bombay,' the money in trust with the East India Company's bankers.

Mary had two brothers: Hugh Reginald, author and musician, Thomas Willyams, Midshipman R.N. who emigrated to Melbourne, Australia, and one sister Margaret Elizabeth.

By the time her sons, Camborne and Hugh were 11 and 10 Mary Paynter was a widow, and did her best to bring up her family with high standards. Later on she tried to discourage friendships with the sons of a distant relation George Paynter because his family were so wealthy, and she felt it would be a bad influence on them.

She worked in the East end of London to improve the lot of poor people. Even in writing her family history she was kindly disposed to people. I am grateful to her for those writings and to Sonya for allowing me to read them a few years ago. My father remembered her, and said once what a good woman she was.

At Boskenna on a dull winter evening she would assemble in the Hall those who were musically inclined, herself on the piano, the butler Aukett on the violin, a maid on the flute, and with others play easy arrangements of the classics.
(More details of her in the next chapter).

Mary Davies Paynter's funeral

Mary died at Brighton and the funeral was at St.Buryan. On the coffin was the inscription; Mary Davies Paynter, died 15th May, 1905, aged 68.

The funeral was conducted by the Rector Canon Martyn, and the organist was J.W.Stone. The hymn ' The homeland', was sung. It was written by Mary's brother, Hugh Reginald Haweis, and set to music by Sir Arthur Sullivan, and was much sung at funerals and was in the old Methodist Hymnbook. The first verse is as follows:-

> *The homeland! The homeland! The land of the freeborn;*
> *There's no night in the homeland, But aye the fadeless morn,*
> *I'm sighing for the homeland, My heart is aching here;*
> *There's no pain in the homeland, To which I'm drawing near.*

The chief mourners were Col and Mrs.Paynter, elder son and wife, Mrs.Hugh Paynter daughter-in-law , Mr.G.Aukett (butler), Mr.J.Collins (head gardener), Miss Young and Miss White (employees), Mr.G.R.Polgrean (clerk), and workmen also followed the coffin.

Amongst those present were Dr.Montgomerie, Major Harvey, Mr.Walter Borlase, Mr.J.Trelawny, Rev Stona, Dr.Jago, Mrs. and Miss A.Martyn, Rev.A.Tonkin of Treverven, Messrs. R.Tonkin, P,Jelbart, H.H.Laity, J.Lugg, H.Care, J.Pengelly, J.Rowe, J.Williams G.Prowse, E.Prowse. J.Hosking, R.Harry, J.Mann C.C., J.Thomas, H. and T.Woolcock, A.Hosking, V.Care, A.Mann, W.Jeffery, H.Laity, J.Richards, J.Matthews, E.Jackson, W Clemens, and others. Her son Mr.Hugh Paynter was in America.

Her Will 1905

She left her son Col.Paynter Trewoofe, Tregadgwith, and Clapper Mill, also £2,400 secured on a mortgage on Alsia Farm, and £838 in Consols Stock.

She left certain Stocks and Securities to her second son Hugh, and a legacy to her daughter-in-law Beatrice Louise Paynter, Hugh's wife, and to their children Ann, Donnett, and Thomas £50 each.

Most of this property and stocks had been her marriage settlement in 1858 from her father-in-law Thomas Paynter.

Remember the Lady in White, the ghost of Ann , and the curse of the old nurse that there would never be another daughter born here. There never was. After three generations of sons only, came Betty and her two cousins, but none were born at Boskenna!

Chapter 9

CAMBORNE HAWEIS PAYNTER (Col. Paynter) 1864 – 1949

Camborne Haweis Paynter, elder son of Reginald Hearle Paynter and Mary Davies Haweis was born on 25 Jan. 1864 in or near London. His younger brother Hugh Haweis Paynter was born on 14 Nov. 1865. Camborne was 11 when his father died. From then on he was very much "the man of the house". His grandfather

BOSKENNA HOME FARM Henry and Mary Ann Care with Annie and Charlie Johns, Johnny Williams, Will Stone, Dick Stone and boy Williams.

Thomas died in 1863 a year before he was born. His only Paynter uncle Camborne Hastings was killed at Newcastle on Tyne while assisting at the Great Fire in 1854. He had no first or second cousins on the Paynter side of the family. His grandmother Ann had two brothers, the elder was Charles Moody of Kingston in Somerset, and for some years M.P. for Somerset. He had no children. He made Camborne his heir. The younger brother William Moody remained single, and left his money chiefly to Hugh, Camborne's brother.

Camborne was educated at Charterhouse in Surrey. He entered School in Oration Quarter (autumn term) 1877 and left in Cricket Quarter (summer) 1882.

The Form lists for his last year there show that he was top in the autumn of 1881, then half way down in the two following terms. He represented his house at tennis. He was in the boarding House known as Pageites. Little is recorded of his early years. In 1883 he spent Christmas at Boskenna, perhaps a new experience for him. John Collins, who came down from Devon and became a gardener, clouted him as a boy when his mother Mrs. Mary Paynter requested it.

George Aukett, the butler

Mr Aukett, later the butler at Boskenna, first met Camborne and Hugh when he was at West Slaugham in the service of Canon Haweis, Camborne's grandfather. Aukett relates in his notes how he travelled on the "Flying Dutchman" train to Penzance, arriving at about 8.45 pm, and was met by John Collins the gardener who took him to Boskenna. Canon Haweis and his daughter, Mary Paynter, Camborne's mother, were proceeding to Penzance in easy stages from Sussex with a Wagonette, and arriving there to put up at the Mounts Bay Hotel, while workmen were finishing rebuilding Boskenna.

Henry Care and Mary Ann

On arrival at Boskenna, Aukett was met by Henry Care (who was farming at Boskenna at the time) and Mr Vennicombe, foreman of the works. They welcomed him warmly. Aukett told the story about Henry Care, a kindly old man, who, on his return from market with Mary Ann his wife, had the bad luck to be thrown out of their cart. He said *"How could I help it, my dear,? I had the reins in one hand, and the whip in the other, and a pair of boots in the other, so how could I help it?"*. (They were my great grandparents. More of them later).

Aukett was entertained at the farmhouse until the mansion was ready, and Mary Ann told him many tales of the Paynter family. In fact the Cares entertained guests of the Paynters whenever the big house was closed up.

JOHN COLLINS, gardener and mason, and GEORGE AUKETT, butler, longest serving employees of COL. PAYNTER (seated).

43

Secret room

An interesting story tells of a visitor, Miss Gawthrop, (later Mrs Lional Tertis), walking around the grounds one morning in 1886, noticing a window she could not account for. This caused great excitement, a wall was demolished to reveal an alcove precisely the same as the dining room below, subsequently it became known as the priest's hiding-place.

The young Squire

The year 1885 was to be an important one for Camborne. On his 21st birthday he inherited 2000 acres from Grandfather Thomas Paynter, and a fortune left by Charles Moody. Camborne, (who was to be the last of the male line to live at Boskenna), did not live there during his childhood. A caretaker in the later period was suspected of having sold valuable items from the house. When at last Camborne came he built a large extension to the house and an east wing was added. Stone was used from engine houses at Balswidden, St.Just. Over the door of the drawing room are the words "restored 1886."

This room was intended to be the front hall. The smoking room was rebuilt at the same time. Also the billiard room and the rooms above. Tom Paynter, Camborne's nephew has written *" The present house is a mixture of several periods. The library is panelled with wood from a ship of the Armada."*

Cornishman   22 October 1885

' The oldest portion of the mansion of Boskenna has been recently pulled down, and it is intended to raise upon the site an improved and more imposing structure.

During the demolition several unexpected remains of old work has come to light. One, which was overlaid with a plaster partition and a modern mantelpiece, is a large open fire formed by jambs and lintel composed of granite, in three massive slabs, with moulded front and a boss and star ornament on the base on either side. Two or three mullion windows, more or less perfect, have been discovered, walled up and covered over, besides several fragments of larger windows. These wrought stones have been found in the thick walls utilised as ordinary building material. An arched doorway of worked granite was also found walled up and covered over. Although the portion of the house now taken down was considered the oldest part, it evidently was a successor of a far superior building, which must have been allowed to become a ruin; as to its south front, at least being built in a style unworthy of the older house; or it may be that alterations from time to time - perhaps so-called restoration - may have affected the degradation. The wrought stones now brought to light will, as far as possible, be fitted together and worked into the new building'.

On the lawn at Boskenna is an inscribed tombstone of a Roman soldier. It was discovered by the late Canon Martyn near Tregadgwith, when being used as a gate post.

More of Mary Davies Paynter

Camborne's mother, Mary Davies Paynter managed the estate while her son was in the Army. The house had been much neglected. It had not been occupied by the family for years. Now it was being rebuilt. Money was not always made available, as being in the 5th Dragoons was, for Camborne, an expensive way of living and he did not always know what was going on at home. At one time Mary found it so hard to keep the house going that she went to live in the village. She rescued and restored some beautiful tapestries of the Mary Stuart period which she found in rags in the attic.

Army Career

Lieutenant Colonel Camborne Haweis Paynter, (or Col. Paynter as I shall now call him), was commissioned into the 21st Hussars in 1884, and later that year transferred to the 5th Dragoon Guards, promoted captain in 1889, and major when he was transferred to the 6th Inniskilling Dragoons in 1890. (When the local people of Lamorna heard that Colonel Paynter was in the Inniskilling Dragoons they were very upset thinking he had turned Catholic, and they burnt an effigy of him. Colonel's mother called the people of Lamorna together and told them in no uncertain terms that her son was Protestant and would remain so). After serving in the South African War where, according to his mother, he served in the Royal Monmouth Engineers, he returned to Cornwall. In 1905, in his mother's will, he is referred to as being in the Militia Forces, which I presume to mean he was not then in the regular army but could be called on in an emergency. In the 1914 War he was Major in the 1st Devon Yeomanry, commanded a Remount Depot, and then served as Town Major in France. He also became Honorary Colonel of more than one Territorial Unit.

Electricity, First in Cornwall

About the year 1899 the telephone was installed and poles were erected to St. Buryan. Mr. Aukett, in his notes, writes about the installation of electricity at Boskenna about 1900, the first house in Cornwall. Lights also were erected outside including those to the stables. This work was completed by Hugh Paynter, assisted by John Collins who thought Hugh was amazing! John would proudly show people around who came to see this wonderful installation. He remarked to Aukett, *"After it was finished do you know, Mr George, I could not for the life of me see where I could light it with a match!*

Early Motor Car

Col. Paynter, ahead of his time, brought the first car to West Cornwall about 1903, a steam driven Serpolet, AF2. When he drove it at night, with a red glow from the furnace, some old people at first thought he was in league with The Devil. Perhaps

His Honour J.W.Scobell Armstrong thought so too, *"My first drive in a motorcar was along the road by the sea between Penzance and Marazion. The car was a Serpolet, an open contraption with seats on the top of a receptacle that seemingly contained a quantity of powerful machinery. It actually reached, between Penzance and Long Rock, the appalling speed of thirty miles an hour. I clung to my seat expecting every moment to be my last"!*

At times the car would break down and my great uncle, Vivian Care of Downs Barn, would get very exasperated when he was sent for to tow it home with his horse.

Tenants' Dinner

Mr. Aukett wrote about the Court Dinner, an important function, at which the estate farmers under the supervision of Col. Paynter's agent Mr. Roscorla paid their rent direct to the Colonel, who then entertained them all to dinner in his dining room

Later one of the party was called upon to say grace:-

> *"The Lord be praised,*
> *My belly's raised*
> *One inch above the table,*
> *And I be blowed,*
> *If I ain't stowed*
> *As much as I am able!"*

There were songs and speeches and thanks and loud cheers for the Colonel.

Brass Band

Another event was the visit of Buryan Brass Band on Christmas morning who, after they had performed, were invited into the house and given breakfast, and one of the band, possibly John Stone, would entertain the company by singing "Jeremiah, blow the fire." with much humour. They were probably a little merry after spending the night playing carols at the farm houses and being entertained (I remember them coming to my home at Boskennal in the early 1930s when I was a small child, and being amazed to hear them performing in the middle of the night!)

Gypsies

Another group who were welcome at Boskenna were the gypsies. Apparently the Paynter family had at one time done the gypsies a good turn and they never forgot it.

Headless Ghost

Perhaps the St Buryan Brass Band was fortunate that none of them met the headless ghost who had been seen only recently in the back-drive! The legend is that he carries his head under his arm, and if you should meet him he will throw his head at you. If he does you will die within the year! One morning the old postman Campbell arrived there in a bad way. He was white as a sheet and terrified. He had met the headless ghost! He died within the year. Had he really met the ghost, or was it a prankster?

Hugh Haweis Paynter.

Colonel Paynter's brother Hugh was born on the 14th November 1865. He was a Naval Cadet at 13 years, Midshipman at 15, in H.M.S. Northumberland at 16, and in the Egyptian War at 17.

Highly intelligent, he left the navy and took a degree in engineering. He became a mining consultant engineer, practising in South Africa, Australia and China. He worked for Armstrong Whitworth on the Tyne, and was responsible for Paravane, a device used to cut anchors of moored mines. He travelled all over Europe for the firm and was their representative with the Grand Fleet. He also carried out a propaganda tour with Lord Northcliffe in America and Russia. Among the medals he received were the Order of the Rising Sun, Japan and the Order of the Medjadie Turkey. On several occasions he took full (though unofficial) charge of the London to Brighton Coach.

Cruiser to Japan

Commander Hugh Paynter R.N. was commissioned to secretly deliver one of two cruisers, the Kasuga, in January 1904, to Japan from Genoa in Italy. Col. Paynter, or Major as he was then, went with him as gunner and to impose discipline, for the crew were a motley crowd of men picked up in the docks. There was no British Naval disciplinary code to fall back on, as they were flying the Japanese flag and had 'shot in the locker', at a time when Japan was at war with Russia. (Britain feared Russian expansion and were allied with Japan).

The two Kasuga class armoured cruisers, the Kasuga and the Nisshin, were originally laid down for the Italian Navy, but bought by Argentina for the war against Chile after they were launched. The war ended and Argentina sold them to Japan who wished to match the Russian fleet.

Both the Kasuga and the Nisshin were completed on 7 January 1904, and immediately they were loaded and set off for Japan. From our local newspaper we read the following, *"The Nisshin and Kasuga, Singapore, Feb. 6. -- The Japanese cruisers Nisshin and Kasuga left at midnight yesterday'. A telegram was received from Tokyo that they must leave before Feb. 6, whether their coaling was complete or not.*

Arrival in Japan

Much interest was felt in West Cornwall in regard to these ships, owing to the fact that Capt. Hugh Paynter had been in charge of the Kasuga, and was accompanied by his brother, Major Paynter, of Boskenna."- Another news item read, *"Honour for Capt. Paynter. (Central News Agency). TOKYO, Tuesday. Captain Lea, Captain Paynter, and Lieut. Boyle, who navigated the Nisshin and Kasuga from Genoa to Japan, were received in audience by the Emperor this morning. His Majesty conferred upon the three officers the fourth class of the Order of the Rising Sun. The Emperor conferred other decorations on the subordinate officers and gave handsome presents to the crews."*-

LIEUTENANT HUGH PAYNTER, the brother of Col. Paynter.

It says something for the personality of both Commander Hugh Paynter and Commander Boyle R.N. who commanded the second ship, that they brought the ships there safely. Not only were they decorated by the Emperor but they were feted throughout the country. Later a Japanese garden was constructed at Boskenna complete with Buddha.

British Neutrality

Soon after the cruisers arrived in Japan the Home Secretary, in the House of Commons, announced a Royal proclamation on neutrality and warned *"all our loving subjects to observe the law of nations against breaking any blockade established by belligerent powers. For carrying officers, soldiers, despatches, arms, ammunitions, would incur the government's high displeasure!* After this diplomatic hypocrisy there was a furore in Parliament when a member of the House of Lords raised a question on the subject! While the Royal Cornwall Gazette appears to have made no mention to the British connection, they did report in their overseas news that the Kasuga and the Nisshin were despatched to Russian occupied territory near Port Arthur. There they made indirect bombardment for two hours. The two forts there were silenced. The two cruisers had a vital affect on the War which was won mainly at sea. (The Kasuga was used as a training ship in the 1920s and was scrapped in 1948).

Speeches in the House of Lords 25 February 1904
THE WAR AND THE BRITISH NAVY (Hansard)

Earl SPENCER: *My Lords, I wish to ask the First Lord of the Admiralty a Question of which I have given him private notice. It is one of great moment to this country, and the points contained in it are now creating considerable interest everywhere. I wish to know whether the noble Earl can give any information as to the following statements which have been made to the press and elsewhere as to the action of this country in matters affecting the Russo-Japanese War, and which is interpreted as evidence that this country has broken the letter or the spirit of the law of neutrality: (1) in allowing the Argentine cruisers bought by Japan to leave Genoa under the Red Ensign; (2) in supplying naval officers to man these vessels; (3) in escorting these cruisers in the Mediterranean by His Majesty's ship.*

KASUGA CRUISER. Secretly delivered to Japan from Genoa by Hugh Paynter and Col. Paynter with a motley crew.

The First Lord of the Admiralty (The EARL of SELBORNE):*"My Lords, I recognise the gravity of the questions put to me by my noble friend. I am absolutely at a loss to conjecture from what source these stories have emanated. There is, I fear some influence at work which is endeavouring to misrepresent the attitude of this country and to show that the Navy is not observing that strict*

LIEUTENANT HUGH PAYNTER BEING ENTERTAINED IN JAPAN (in centre wearing decoration).

TREVELLAN, LAMORNA, built 1935

ANN DAKIN with horse and trap at Trevellan

DONNETT PAYNTER with converted ambulance on active service in France.

neutrality which is incumbent upon it. I will take each of the points in turn mentioned by the noble Earl. It has been stated that the two cruisers bought by the Japanese Government from the Argentine Government, and which were built in Genoa, were allowed to leave that port under a British flag. My Lords there is not a word of truth in that statement. An application as made to the Consulate, the ships be allowed to fly the British flag. The request was immediately refused, and they never flew that flag for one second.

Again, it has been stated that the Admiralty supplied two naval officers as captains of these cruisers. Again there is not a word of truth in that statement. Two gentlemen who had been officers in the Navy were selected by the Japanese Government to command these cruisers. They were gentlemen over whom the Admiralty had no sort of control whatever, and they drew neither pay nor pension from the Government. They had, however, some time ago, voluntarily placed themselves on what is known as the emergency list of ex-officers who are available for service in time of war. The moment the Admiralty learnt that these officers, over whom they have no control, but were on this emergency list, had undertaken to command these cruisers, the Board decided to strike them off the emergency list; and this was done before any kind of complaint was made, before the facts became public, and simply because the Board of Admiralty thought it the wiser course to do that which would leave no room for misrepresentation. The third statement that has been made is that these cruisers, after leaving Genoa, were escorted through the Mediterranean by his Majesty's ships. There is no foundation of any sort or kind for that statement. I do not know what colourable accident may have given rise to it. I do not believe myself, and have no knowledge, that they were even sighted by any of His Majesty's ships".

The family of Hugh Paynter

Hugh, who died in 1934, married Beatrice Louisa Barkworth of Oxted in Surrey 1890. She was well read and musical and of an unselfish disposition. In the First War she helped found and finance and run the first Royal Flying Corps Hospital. At one time she was in charge of the forces hospital at Heligan, lent by Capt. Tremayne, in Cornwall. Hugh and she had three children,-

1 Ann, born 1892 was a lifelong supporter of the Scout and Guide movement, a talented horsewoman and rider. While in Winchelsea, Sussex, she not only formed a successful Guide troupe, but also a Physical Training Club for boys and one for young men. She formed a troupe of about 30 guides at St Buryan in 1938.

Ann married Capt. Geoffrey Dakin of Lucas Green Manor, Surrey. His health was wrecked by The War and he died in 1931. Col. Paynter called her his favourite niece, and later gave her eleven acres of land near Lamorna stipulating that she must not have a circus or fairground! In 1935 she built a house there 'Trevellen,' (mention is made of her later in David Evans' recollections). She adopted Paul Dakin aged 10 in 1947. Both she and her sister Donnett were presented at court.

2 In the First World War Donnett (born 1894) drove an ambulance (converted from her father's own limousine). She served in France for three years and suffered from the effects of mustard gas, and was twice mentioned in despatches. After the war she became a competent musician. She died in 1921 aged 27.

3 Tom was born 1901 at Rye. In 1915 he won a scholarship to enter the prestigious public school of Repton. Revd. Fisher, headmaster, (later Archbishop of Canterbury), wrote, "Dear Mr. Paynter, I am glad to tell you that we have today elected your boy to a scholarship. He was comfortably top of the list". From a boy he composed and performed music in public. His composition of The Newlyn Suite was performed by the Penzance Orchestral Society in 1946 in St. John's Hall and was a great success.

A bachelor he became an expert skier. He wrote an interesting book in 1954 - 'The Ski and the Mountain'. He was a Commando Major and was in the Lovat Scouts in Canada during the Second World War, and became a qualified architect. Tom retired eventually to Sellan Mill, Sancreed, and died in 1976. He was the Paynter family Archivist and his work- 'A Parcel of Cornish Lawyers' has been a great help in compiling this book.

Son and Heir

Tom wrote that before going to war in South African in 1899 Colonel Paynter desired that his brother Hugh, should have a son to carry on Colonel's estate. Hugh duly obliged, but Colonel married in 1904 at the age of 40 and produced an heir in 1907.

Recollections of a young man

Ann was married to a Geoffrey Dakin who died in 1930. She was childless and after his death, lived at Steeple Bumstead, Essex, and at Winchelsea in East Sussex, before coming to live in Lamorna, where she had Trevellen built for her. She had a small holding and kept goats. She had a regular helper named Jenkin and kept a horse and a pony. From time to time another helper, Jelbert from Newlyn would turn up with a horse and cart full of children and some implements, to do cultivation.

She also played violin in the Penzance Orchestra under Morgan Hosking. She had a rather splendid Amati violin, which she ultimately sold. I was going up to London at the time, so she asked me to take it up with me in the train,: I was to leave it in a lockup luggage bay for Christies to collect, which I did! I didn't dare take my eyes off it for the whole journey.

In about 1947, Mrs Ann Dakin adopted a son, Paul. He and I became great friends, so I got to know her and Tom Paynter (I was allowed to call him Uncle Tom, although he was no relation of mine). They both gave the impression of being rather reserved, but when one got to know them, they could be very amusing. Many times I remember having tea with them all at Trevellen and laughing until the tears ran down our cheeks. We also played Racing Demon, which was quite hilarious. Tom and Ann were both good, kind people. She had many good qualities, but tolerance was not one of them. She detested Roman Catholicism. When Betty Paynter became a Roman Catholic, they never saw each other again. Subsequently, Tom Paynter and Ann Dakin lived at Sellan Mill, Sancreed.

I have many memories of Mrs Ann Dakin. She used to take us over to Kennack Sands to bathe, and I remember just before Christmas 1958, going with her in her pony and trap round the village of Paul, delivering her Christmas presents.

Colonel Paynter marries

In October 1904 Colonel Paynter married Ethel Nina Patience, many years his junior, only daughter of Sir Edgcombe Venning, FRCS, of Cadogan Place, London, Surgeon to Edward VII. Sir Edgecombe had performed an appendix operation on King Edward VII just before his Coronation which had to be postponed. He later retired to Falmouth. Ethel's eldest brother was killed in India, (where he held a Government appointment), whilst elephant hunting in 1897. (The appendix operation was the first ever performed). The following was written by Anne Johns of St Loy maybe from an old newspaper cutting,-- "<u>An Old Home</u>. *Major Paynter and his pretty bride, who was Miss Ethel Venning motored down to Cornwall on Sunday to Boskenna, Major's old home, which has been in his family since 1600, and the lovely gardens which overlook the sea. Miss Venning was one of the prettiest brides of the week in her Romney frock with roses and lace, and her 400 wedding gifts include a ruby and pearl stomacher and a diamond ring among others from her parents. A 24 horsepower motor from Major Paynter, while Miss*

Venning's present to him was a lovely miniature of herself. The Duke and Duchess Buccleach gave a diamond bracelet and the Marchioness of Devonshire (her godmother) also sent a handsome gift."

Mrs. Ethel Nina Paynter.

Mrs. Paynter had many interests. A keen gardener she wrote a "Children's Book of Gardening" in conjunction with Mrs Alfred Sidgewick. She bought a Queen Ann cabinet with the profits from the book.

A new school was built at St Buryan in 1910 at a cost of £1600. A great day it was for the children on Monday October 3rd. when they marched up from the old school into the new one. On the following Friday Mrs Paynter, Chairman of the Managers, gave all the children a 'tea treat'. She inspected the school regularly until 1922. My grandfather, Augustus Hosking, was her deputy until 1920 when he died,

While her husband was in France during the First World War she helped to run the estate. When a young lad on the estate said he was too young to plough she showed him how by taking the reins and ploughing across the field herself! Mrs.Paynter loved the Rockery, or as it was later known, the Japanese Garden. She spent many hours and a lot of money to make it beautiful, planting cherry trees and rare plants. She created paths so that its beauty could be seen from any angle, and had a bridge built so that people could pass over to the centre of the pond where on a mound was a Buddha model. She had garden seats placed around, one she named 'The Seat of Great Men' It had a small lawn in front. The Rockery was a natural 'love tryst'. Perhaps one of the 'great men' was Lamorna Birch .He had made sketches there for his painting, The Garden of the Little Buddha, and in February 1925 was working on it for the summer exhibition. He was very tired and remarked "It seems I shall never get this canvas covered!"

ETHEL NINA PATIENCE PAYNTER
nee VENNING

55

Social Events and Tea Treats

Mrs Paynter was a leader of fashion and entertained freely at Boskenna. It was reported that six duchesses were expected one weekend. With her husband escorting her she would attend social events such as the Helston Flora where the ladies wore, and still wear, long dresses of high fashion, and the men wear top hats and morning suits. Over the years there were many social events at Boskenna including garden fetes which Mrs.Paynter organised for the St.Buryan Nursing Association. Mrs.Susie Mitchell, in her "Recollections of Lamorna" wrote, *"The Church School treat was a visit to Boskenna House; invited by Col. and Mrs.Paynter for tea and games on their terraced lawn. They also provided a swing among the trees and we spent many happy hours there".* Walter Grose once said, *"We also went there from St. Buryan School. Col. and Mrs.Paynter were like kings and queens to us".* I also recall being enrolled as a Boy Scout on the lawn there, with others, before Commissioner Venning, Mrs.Paynter's brother, in 1939/40.

SHIPWRECKS AT ST. LOY, 1912. (From local newspapers.)

The steamer South America, 4197 tons, commanded by Capt. F. Bowling, on a voyage from Hamburg to Cardiff in ballast, went ashore in Boskenna Bay near Lamorna, at 1.30 this morning (13 March). By the presence of mind and prompt action of two men living near the spot all the crew, 36 men and the Captain's wife and son were saved. The sound of the ship's siren and the rockets awakened Mr. Jimmy Richards who was first on the scene. He found a large steamer standing upright on the rocks not more than 50 yards from the shore. With great presence of mind he waved his brightly lit lantern, and hailing those on board, he was able to give them advice as to the landing of the crew by means of the boats. Mr. C. Trewern of St. Loy arrived and at Mr. Richards suggestion he cycled to Mousehole to summon the Life Saving Apparatus, after attempts to get through by telephone failed. Mr. Richards shouted to the crew to launch a boat and row towards him. Mr. Read, the second officer, took charge of the lifeboat, which took aboard 16 of the shipwrecked crew, including the captain's wife. It was some time before Mrs. Bowling could be persuaded to face the ordeal of clambering down the ship's side. Guided by Mr. Richards and his lantern, the men pulled for the shore. with great difficulty they guided the boat between the rocks, and everyone got drenched. The other boat was launched and the remaining 22 hands got taken off. Mrs. Bowling was taken to the house of Mrs. Johns, where she was well cared for. Mrs. Johns had also been down showing the way across the rocks with her wooden lantern. Her photo was in the papers with her lamp. The Captain's wife stayed with her a day or two, and gave her lovely presents for her kindness to them. About 20 of the crew went to Col. Paynter's where they were given a good breakfast, while some

The SOUTH AMERICA ashore at St. Loy, March 1912, also the ABERTAY, wrecked alongside there, October 1912.

went to Mr. Richards. He was presented later with a handsome barometer with the inscription, *"-- largely as a result of his skilful efforts under adverse conditions, the shipwrecked crew were enabled to effect a safe landing"*.

(Jimmy Richards was my great uncle, more of him later).

Salvage

I have heard that farmers gave up working the threshing machine at Roslucombe Farm, St.Buryan for a day or two at that time to go down to St.Loy to help with salvage.

Referring to the South America Mr. J. H. Care wrote, *"I stood on the rocks of the bay at St. Loy and saw the auction of the wood that my father and many others had saved and put back away from the waves. The auctioneer gave those who had saved the wood the first chance to buy. The hatchways were made into lovely divisions in the cattle houses at Downs Barn and my uncle Augustus from*

Boskennal Farm had a pitch pine cupboard made from one of the masts. After that the rest of the boat was salvaged and the man in charge was Mr. Slade, who afterwards started the firm of Slade and Co., for many years of Hayle, but at that time he stayed with Mr. Harry Gwennap of Treverven Farm, St. Buryan". The company in charge of the salvage was the Western Marine Salvage Co. (The great grandson of Augustus Hosking, Norman Truscott, was still using the cupboard until recently.)

Mr Harry Gwennap's father, Mr. Tom Gwennap, was asked to supply horses to transfer the salvage to Trevedran Farm at 15 pence a ton, but agreed to do it at 18 pence.

Wreck of the Abertay

In the same year, October 1912, the French steamer Abertay, 599 tons, of Lorient, bound for Barry with pit props, went ashore at St. Loy and berthed alongside the South America in thick fog. From the foredeck a ladder was thrown across to the big steamer, upon which several of the crew clambered carrying a

The CREW of the ABERTAY

lighted lantern. Mr. Jimmy Richards again went down to the water's edge, no mean feat for a man of 60 climbing over big boulders in the dark. With the rising tide the sea continually broke over the steamer, and seeing help was needed, Mr. Richards hastened to the post office at St. Buryan and sent a message for the Newlyn lifeboat.

The ABERTAY, painted by Lamorna Birch.

Mr.Trembath of the Picturedrome made a film of the wreck which he showed the following week. (The Picturedrome had been the Central Hall in Parade St. Penzance. Later it became the Regal Cinema, and finally the Job Centre).

JIMMY (left) helped rescue the crew of the South America, with his brother W.H. Care from Australia. The BAROMETER was awarded to JIMMY RICHARDS for rescuing the crew.

Lamorna Birch also painted the wreck of the Abertay at St.Loy

A special direct telephone line was installed from Boskenna to the Captain of Coast Guards so the signals of ships in trouble could be reported before they struck.

Other wrecks have been recorded in the area in the past. Seven bodies were washed up in one night on the 18th December 1858 when the Isabella from Plymouth was wrecked at St.Loy.

There was another wreck there in 1896, and the remains were an attraction to tourists for many months.

Greek schooner nearly wrecked

A Greek schooner Eulogia Maniatis was nearly wrecked in the same area on Tuesday 22 December 1925.

Mr Ernie Hitchens of St.Dellan went down from his house to put away some potatoes in his barn. Soon afterwards his wife called out that there was a vessel in difficulties, and looking seaward he saw this schooner lying 200/300 yards from the rocks. A small boat containing 4 people was being rapidly rowed landwards. They were in great danger but eventually Ernie managed to get a rope to them and between them they dragged the boat ashore.

ANNIE JOHNS who cared for Capt. Bowling,
his wife and son, after the shipwreck, with
MARY CARE of Boskenna Home Farm.

Mr.W.H.Penrose had also seen the schooner and saw one of the crew loading bundles into the dinghy. He sent word to Mrs. Paynter at Boskenna House, who ordered that they should be brought up there.

This 100 ton schooner, a converted yacht with an auxiliary engine, had left Charlestown in Cornwall loaded with china clay four days before heading for France. Having lost sails and the boom and leaking badly she found herself off the Cornish coast.

On Wednesday 23 December the Eulogia Maniatis was towed clear of Boskenna, and brought safely into Penzance. By 13 January she was still busily discharging her clay cargo prior to undergoing repairs.

Boskenna Bay

In the 1880s a steamer named Boskenna Bay, registered in Cardiff, regularly loaded grain from ports in the Black Sea.

In 1892 Foreshore rights at Boskenna were granted to Col. Paynter by the Prince of Wales, later King Edward VII. Not for the first time, I believe, these rights had been granted to the Paynter family.

During the Second World War a Naval boat was wrecked at St.Loy and Col. Paynter claimed salvage rights. The Admiralty allowed him to take only anything that was floating loose in the water.

St. Loy and St. Dellan.

The bay to the west of Boscawen point is called St. Loy or Boskenna Bay. On land this is divided into three areas - Paynters Cove, St Loy, and St. Dellan.

Paynters Cove which is nearest Boscawen Point has a small swimming pool cut in the rock into which, of recent years, a boulder has rolled.

At St.Loy there was a medieval chapel called St. Loy, but this disappeared a long time ago.

St.Dellan is a small tenement of 11 acres beautifully maintained by the owners Mr and Mrs.John Phillips. This is to the west of the stream that divides Boskenna from Trevedran, and was part of Trevedran and owned by the Vyvyan family for more than 700 years until June 1938 when Sir Courtney Vyvyan sold it all to Colonel Paynter. (That stream and its banks had been 'streamed' for tin before 1500.)

Here also was a medieval chapel called St.Dellan the remains of which were thrown into the sea, including a wrought stone altar, by the then tenant about 1855 without permission of his landlord. It was done to make his turnip patch bigger! The chapel was 37' by 14'. Charles Henderson tells us that Borlase, in his Age of the Saints, described it wrongly as St Loy's Chapel. A field nearby had the name Chapel field. He also states that, in a list of the lands of Ralph Vyvyan "felon "1387, mention is made of Trevydryn and a rent from Sendelowe. Many others have confused St. Loy Chapel with St. Dellan.

A Fire at Boskenna

There was a fire in the Drawing room at Boskenna. The year I know not ,but I believe before 1904, as it appears to have been when Colonel's mother was in residence. She was sorting out a drawer of bills and papers, some of which she threw in the fireplace. A spark, or falling log ignited the paper, which set fire to the old oak mantelpiece and travelled up to the wooden ceiling above. George Aukett the butler recalls the event. *"I was awakened from my sleep, by the ringing of the house bell by one of the maidservants. I put on my slippers and soon found the cause of the alarm. I quickly made my way to the Home Farm and awakened the inhabitants, who, headed by Mr Jimmy Richards with a plate of salt, came to my assistance. With my improvised fire brigade I attempted to put out the fire. By this time the fire had burnt a hole in the ceiling, and having told one or two helpers to swamp the floors with buckets of water, the housemaid in her night attire, in an endeavour to rescue a chair, received the contents of one of the aforesaid buckets, an ablution she did not relish!*

I, in my turn, nearly came to grief in attempting to save the portrait of a Mrs. Paynter by Opie; the fire having burnt a hole in the floor on which I placed my steps in order to reach the picture, I was precipitated with the steps to the ground! It was fortunate that the walls on either side of the fireplace were not lathe and plaster, or the mansion would probably have been doomed.

Water Supply

Aukett wrote about the water supply to the house. *"The first means employed was by a pump from a well, worked by William Angwin, from which he filled two tanks. The supply often proved inadequate, generally running short on a Sunday morning, when there was no one to pump the water. In order to improve the supply , first a hydraulic ram, then a windmill, was brought into action, and subsequently a 5 horse power engine was established. These provided our old friend John Collins with many excursions to and fro, to keep one or the other of the three in working order. The water came from a spring which has never been known to run dry, and Mrs. Care told me that in order to preserve his rights, the Lord of the Manor exacted two peppercorns per annum."*

There was an elaborate system of pumps to supply water around Boskenna estate and also around Lamorna. Mr. John Phillips of St. Dellan still receives water from that supply to this day. For Lamorna there was a wind pump on Tregurno cliffs and a ram pump to supplement it. There was also a water supply in Borah Moor. Some of this is of a later date. Colonel must have had one of the earliest tractors in Cornwall. It would have been a Fordson on iron wheels, and no rubber tyres. (Tom Gwennap tells me that in 1918 or 1919 his traction engine was condemned, and they hired Colonel's tractor to drive the threshing machine. On one occasion while threshing the tractor backfired, and a workman jumped off the machine in fright. Only a year or two previously a steam engine had blown up at Banns Farm, St. Buryan, killing one man).

Managing Boskenna

Major Gilbert Evans, of whom we shall read more later, was agent to Col. Paynter for a while up to 1914, and later on Mr H. Laity, farming at Tregiffian Farm, helped supervise the estate. Colonel was progressive with his ideas.

Boskenna Football Club

Before the First World War the Boskenna Football Club was formed. On a printed card was written 'President: Col. C.H.Paynter, Vice Presidents: Capt. C.G.Evans, The Revd. A Cornish, Captain: C.W.Clark, Vice Captain: J.W.Jarvis, Hon. Sec. and Treasurer: C.Clark,
Colours; Yellow and Amber.
Ground: Boskenna.

Lamorna and the artists

Lamorna was Col.Paynter's pride and joy. He set out to improve his estate which included Lamorna Cove and the properties on the west side of Lamorna river, and built studios and garages, and also some houses.

Here I would like to quote a paragraph from Austin Wormleighton's book, A PAINTER LAUREATE

Lamorna was typical of the changing face of English village life. In the nineteenth century, agricultural workers had drifted from the countryside towards the towns as farming became less profitable. The influence of the landed class was in decline, and estate owners such as Col. Paynter faced a choice of adapting to modern circumstances or clinging to the old order and seeing their estates broken up and disintegrate. Paynter set out radically to change the complexion of the estate. He introduced a five and a half day week for all his workers, giving them a

free Saturday afternoon long before it became the normal practice. His brief friendship with the Marriotts had given him a special liking for writers and painters. They brought colour, intellect and style to the remote and backward-looking community and Paynter was happy to build and adapt properties for their use. In this way, he had a strong influence on the early development of Lamorna as an artists colony. He was, an eccentric squire, and while he became known for the sureness and fairness of his touch in community matters, his actions as a landlord were not always calculated to make or improve friendships. For a time he insisted that all male tenants should have served in the Army; for others there was a stipulation in their leases that they played bridge or that they were not Roman Catholics.

Wormleighton's book tells of Birch wanting to widen the river in front of his studio to create a trout stream .Other painters were willing to help. The job was difficult because of the large boulders. They enlisted the help of Gilbert Evans Col. Paynter's land agent who had been living in Lamorna since 1909. He showed Lamorna Birch how to do it using the help of the artists and other villagers. Gilbert was remembered with great affection, and part of the social life of the artists colony.

New enterprises

Colonel improved the village amenities. At different periods he opened a carpenters shop, cafe, produce shop, and Ark Garage. By 1911 Constable Albert Jewell was living there, Mrs Annie Trewhella ran the Post Office, and a school was opened with 50 pupils under a single mistress Miss Nicholls. (She later married Mr. Richard Yeaman Hosking my great uncle). On Wednesday afternoons Mrs. Paynter came to Lamorna in a pony and jingle with her sewing machine, and helped a group of women with dressmaking and embroidery at the Cliff House Temperance Hotel.

GILBERT EVANS
agent to Col. Paynter
1908 to 1914. Photo
about 1908.

Living pictures

The following is a brief extract from the Cornishman 1910---*"Living Pictures at Lamorna :   On Saturday a very successful entertainment was given at Cliff House, Lamorna in aid of St. Buryan District Nursing Society. The principal feature of the entertainment, which was organised by Mrs Alfred Sidgwick, was a series of living pictures. The tableaux began with a charming picture, entitled "Once upon a time", of a group of children listening to an old fairy story. Another very effective picture was "Motherless," representing a fisherman's cottage where the widowed husband (Mr Lamorna Birch) was with clumsy tenderness nursing his motherless infant. There were several other tableaux and the last one depicted "The Lady With The Lamp," (Miss Zoe Barker), passing through the hospital, as she passes one wounded soldier he kisses the hem of her dress.*
The second part of the programme consisted of a concert. Miss Gotch contributed costume songs, Mr Lamorna Birch and Miss Dorothy Watts were vocalists, Miss Gibbs and Mr Hutchings played two pieces of Chopin, Mr Aukett (the butler) rendered popular ditties with great sense of humour.

Mrs Paynter occupied the chair and thanked the organisers for a very successful entertainment. Among the crowded audience were Mr and Mrs Alfred Sidgwick, Sir Edgcombe and Lady Venning, Mrs T.B.Bolitho, Mr and Mrs Ullman, Mr and Mrs Stanhope Forbes, and Mr and Mrs Knight, who also painted two most attractive picture posters of the entertainment, the sale of which contributed materially to the substantial amount that accrued in aid of the funds of a really useful society."

One day a tramp was posing for Dame Laura Knight at Lamorna almost hidden by rocks, only a handkerchief for covering, when two elderly ladies from Penzance came with hampers and seated themselves on the grass above. Seeing what was going on they complained loudly and were going to stop it, but Colonel (called 'Curl-and-Painter' by the village children), said *"Laura Knight can do what she likes - that piece of shore is my property "*. Colonel owned much of the property on the St Buryan side of the river and built many of the studios as well as some of the houses. After the first World War he named some of the studios after towns in France where he had been 'Town Major', controlling and administering these towns when they were recaptured.

Colonel Paynter once said jokingly to his agent, *"There are so many artist chappies on my land now, Gilbert, you will soon be taking a roll call at sunset!"* He also said, *"Lots of painters but not a decent carpenter in sight! "*

Gilbert Evans and Florence

Alfred Munnings had a stormy relationship with his sensitive wife Florence. She turned to Gilbert Evans for consolation, and he a man of high ideals fell hopelessly in love with her and she with him. In March 1914 Evans left to join the Royal Engineers Survey Department in Nigeria. Arriving in Liverpool he found his ship delayed. So he went down to London to see a painting of Florence in the Royal Academy and by chance met her there. She came back to Lamorna, became

COL. PAYNTER, FAMILY AND STAFF. In the picture are: (standing), D. Wood, John Warren Stone, William C. Lugg, William Mill, Harry Payne, John Collins, Charlie Johns, George Aukett, Chris Jelbart, Johnny Williams, Tom Bailey, John Jarvis, William Penrose, George Polgreen, Jessie Godfrey, Annie Marley, Mrs. Dunstan, Jinny Lugg, Amy Godfrey; (seated) Harry Wharton, Jim Grenfell, Charlie Leah; (on seat) Mrs Paynter, Betty Paynter, Colonel Paynter, Major Evans.

increasingly unhappy in her marriage and took her life. At the inquest Colonel Paynter, the foreman of the jury, returned a verdict of poisoning by cyanide administered by herself during temporary insanity.

The Connection, by David Evans

My father, Charles Gilbert Evans, came from an old family of minor Welsh gentry, who had in the past owned a lot of land outside Cardiff. The elder sons inherited and farmed the land and the younger ones became academics and Anglican Clergymen. My Grandfather, Charles Evans, was the first to enter the professions, and practised as a solicitor in Cardiff. He was also Clerk to The Magistrates in Landaff and president elect of the Law Society in Cardiff when he died in 1907.

After leaving Rugby in 1901 at the age of eighteen, he was commissioned, almost immediately, into the Royal Monmouthshire Royal Engineers Militia, as a Second Lieutenant. Militia Regiments were part-time affairs, where you were recalled for training and regimental activities for a few weeks from time to time, but could do your own thing when not required by the regiment. My father ran a trout farm on the river Monnow, with a brother officer, Truaron Vizzard.

Lt. Col. Camborne Haweis Paynter, joined the Monmouth Militia in 1904, from the Inniskillen Dragoons. My father told a rather amusing story about the Colonel's first day on parade. Officers and men were all assembled in the quadrangle, when Paynter rode in on his horse, dressed in the uniform of the Inniskillen Dragoons, with a plume of feathers on his helmet. (A strange thing to do when joining a new regiment.) A hush descended on the assembled crowd. Lord Raglan, the Colonel of the Regiment, stood there, his moustache bristling, looking somewhat perplexed. My father leant over and whispered to a brother officer - "He looks a bit of a clown to me". Unbeknown to my father, a sergeant who was standing a little further away had overheard this remark, and replied in a much louder voice - "Yes, sir, - He's the clown and we're the b... circus"!

By 1908, the trout farm was not really making enough money to survive on and since my father didn't have much inherited wealth, he was looking around for something to supplement his regimental salary. Paynter, with whom he had now become quite friendly, asked him if he would like to come down to Boskenna to be his agent, while he was making up his mind what he wanted to do with his life.

Capt Gilbert Evans - Colonel Paynter's Agent

On 6th November 1909, my father arrived at Cliff House, the hotel run by Mrs. Jory (now The Lamorna Cove Hotel). He had comfortable rooms there, a bedroom and sitting room overlooking the sea. He was to remain there until April 1914 as the Colonel's agent. He was responsible for the home farm, the flower farm and the packing and transport of the flowers to London. Also the Estate Maintenance staff, and all the tenanted farms, payment of rents and repairs. He had an estate office in Lamorna, known as 'Uncle Tom's Cabin' (it stood where Little Aubawn now stands).

One thing that comes over very clearly from his diaries, is that the Paynters were very kind to him, treating him almost as one of the family. Several times a week he would have lunch with them and was often invited to dinner at Boskenna, not only when the family was there, but to meet guests as well. He was introduced to county society, such as it was in West Cornwall, and remembered going to the coming-out ball held for Mary Bolitho (later Mrs Charles Williams of Trewidden), at Trengwainton.

The Colonel provided a pony for my father's use, but there was evidently no stabling at Cliff House, so he had to keep it at Boskenna. He rode back and forth to Boskenna on a bicycle. Some extracts from my father's diary in his first few days at Boskenna, give some idea of his life there.

His Diary 1909

Mon 8th Nov - Got to Boskenna at about 9.30. Went round finding all the working parties and generally learning the lie of the land, then returned and studied ordnance maps. Saw Nichol, the fishery manager and also the clerk and Paynter later. Lunched at one and back to Boleigh at two. Paynter introduced me to several tenants and showed me round Lamorna. After supper Musgrave (an artist living at Cliff House) took me down to see Lamorna Birch where I also met Hughes, another artist. Liked them both.

Tues 9th Nov - Called at Boleigh on my way to Boskenna and made sundry arrangements. Went all over the place in the morning and in the afternoon went to see Mann (a tenant) at Tregadgwith farm and then on to St Buryan to interview Jarvis, the estate Carpenter. Had tea with Col. and Mrs Paynter.

Weds 10th May - Rode the pony for the first time and she went splendidly; succeed in not being thrown off, Paynter having warned me to be careful!

Mrs Paynter was clearly very fond of him and used to bring down plants from Boskenna and plant them herself in the garden of his office in Lamorna and helped him to choose curtains for his rooms. However, his social life was mostly with the artists. The Birches, the Hughes, Harold and Laura Knight and Alfred and Florence Munnings at Lamorna and The Forbes and the Gotch's at Newlyn.

There are many diary entries. His Mother used to come down from Cardiff from time to time and stayed initially at Cliff House, but later was invited to stay at Boskenna. Being a keen horseman, he took a lot of interest in St. Buryan Races, of which he was Vice President.

My father's developing affection for Florence Munnings caused him eventually to think that he ought to leave. He eventually left to join a Royal Engineers survey party, going out to Nigeria. (See - "Summer in February" by Jonathan Smith .)

The men at Boskenna were obviously very fond of my father and gave him a lovely inscribed silver cigarette case as a leaving present and a farewell tea party. Somewhere I have a list of all those who contributed. Cyril Payne's father (Harry Payne) who was on the staff at Boskenna, used to say that Captain Evans protected them from the Colonel and was very sympathetic to their needs. The Colonel was thought of as a good man, I think, but he was rather eccentric - my father used to call it "Paynterish"!

Alfred Munnings, (later to become Sir Alfred Munnings, President of the Royal Academy) wrote to my father on Sunday 12th April 1914 saying - "Your successor is quite a nice fellow but not the man for the Colonel. He wants a more staid sort of older style I should imagine. Telling us this afternoon that the old devil on the first day, threw a box of flowers out of the packing house at him to catch, which he missed! - and he hasn't told him where a single place is and doesn't know anything".

After The 1914 - 18 War

After the war, my father was seconded to the Colonial service and was in the Survey Department in Nigeria. He came home on leave every three years and always went down to Cornwall and was sometimes invited to stay at Boskenna, which he did. On his promotion to Deputy Surveyor General in 1931, Col Paynter wrote to him as follows:-

"My dear Evans,

Best congratulations on your well deserved promotion. I suppose everyone in Nigeria has to crawl a few miles on his or her stomach before addressing you; how many letters should now be put after your name? Not more I hope, than about 26 or we shall have to use the same ones again"!

In 1933, my father retired to Lamorna with his new bride, 22 years his junior. They went to live at Farrars (now Tregurnow Cliff), a sturdy granite house on the hill directly above Cliff House, which my father had started to build for the Colonel just before the war. Building had stopped during the war, and since it looked like a ruin, it was known as "Tintern Abbey"! My parents became closely involved with the Paynters and social life at Boskenna.

No Popery

Quite early on, my parents went to church at St Buryan. Mr Crofts was now the Rector and he belonged to what is usually known as the Catholic tradition in the Church of England; many Churches in Cornwall belong to it. High Church practices were not to the Colonel's liking! He was sitting just in front of my parents and in the middle of the service, got up, and exclaimed in a loud voice "Damned Popery", and stormed out of the Church, slamming the door with a crash, which reverberated throughout the village. My parents were invited to lunch at Boskenna that day, so off they drove in my father's Armstrong Siddley at the end of the service. "What did you think of the service?" said the Colonel to my mother, on arrival, to which my mother replied "I haven't been to a service like that before, so we just did what Mrs Cousins (who lived at Bodriggy, Lamorna) did." "Oh, don't follow her", said the Colonel, "She's one of the ringleaders"! As far as I know, he never attended St Buryan Church again.

Up to that time Col. and Mrs Paynter used to attend St Buryan Church regularly, sitting in the front pew, he at one end and she at the other. Their only daughter Betty for a while was Sunday School teacher, and gave her class chocolate after the service.

David Evans's brother Tim wrote *" Thereafter he transferred his allegiance to Paul Church where he regularly read the lesson. He read with great expression and I remember particularly an Old Testament lesson when he read of the splattering of the blood of the lambs on the door posts; whereupon a man, (one of the Lugg family I think), had an epileptic fit"!*

69

Mary Ann Care dies

At the beginning of the First War Mrs. Mary Ann Care, my great grandmother, lived in the farmhouse. Her family had farmed Boskenna Home Farm for about 100 years back to her grandparents Mr and Mrs. William Jelbart. She came there in 1830 at about 3 years old and acquired much knowledge of the history of Boskenna. She was often quoted by the Paynters, by Mr. Aukett the butler, and by Mr. James Henry Care her grandson in his writings. He wrote that when the 1914 War broke out, Mary Ann went to Colonel Paynter and asked him to ensure that she should stay at Boskenna Home Farm and die in the old home. *"Mrs. Care"* he said *"I will leave it in black and white, you have done so much for the Paynter family."* In fact, when the Paynters were all away the silver etc. was brought up to the farmhouse and put under the four-poster bed.

Mary Ann had her wish - in 1916 she died in the old home at Boskenna Home Farm at the age of 90..

Richard Richards = Mary Ann = Henry Care, family history

Jimmy Richards (mentioned earlier) was the eldest son of Mary Ann by her first marriage in 1852. As well as both being carpenters he and his brother George produced a lot of early potatoes at St. Loy. The third brother Richard emigrated to New South Wales.

On Mary Ann's second marriage in 1863, this time to Henry Care, they farmed both at Downs Barn, and then Boskenna, farming 200 acres. Her daughter Minnie with her husband Augustus Hosking (my grandparents) with four small children were farming at Trengothal in 1894 when Colonel's mother Mary Davies Paynter called. She said "This kitchen's too small. You had better have Boskennal." This was a farm of over 160 acres of prime land! Minnie's brother William Henry Care emigrated to Melbourne, and her brother Vivian farmed Downs Barn. Vivian's daughter Mary with husband Norman Hosking and son Norman were the last in that family to farm at Boskenna, retiring in 1957.

Your country needs you! 1914 - 18

Mrs. Iris Warren tells me that when war broke out Col. Paynter called a meeting in the village and impressed on the young men that it was their duty to join up and fight for their country against the Germans.. Her brother Edmund Trewhella was one of those who volunteered. He was badly injured in the battle of Vimy Ridge, and never really recovered. He raised 3 sons and died in his fifties One of Colonel's men Charles Johns was deferred for a while because of shortage of staff but eventually he was called up.

St Buryan Races and Denmark

St. Buryan Races were an important event in the area for many years. April 2nd 1891 in the Cornishman we read *"Our local derby came off at St. Buryan on*

Easter Monday. As ever there was a capital attendance of lovers of the turf. The races were run at Downs Barn by kind permission of Mr. Henry Care one of the tenants of Captain Paynter. The ground is high and flat, so admirably adapted for

sharp races, and within a mile is and in an excellent view lay the Atlantic with steamers passing to and fro. The grand stand was filled in no time. Professor Maggs with his Punch and Judy Show provided amusement between the races, also the Buryan Artillery Band was playing sweet music to stimulate the horsemen and to help the

1925 - JACK LEY, JIM GRENFELL, and 3 other employees. *people to forget the cold.*

In 1894 the Boskenna Cup was presented by Capt. Paynter as first prize in a flat race .

As can be seen above St Buryan Races werc taking place in 1891, and went on until 1930 or longer on Easter Monday, usually at Downs Barn. Col. Paynter was president for most of that time followed by his daughter Betty.

Colonel was a fine horseman and an expert on horseflesh. In Ireland while in the Army he won the prestigious Punchestown Cup as a jockey two years running He was a noted rider in steeplechases and at Boskenna bred some famous Westcountry thoroughbreds and racehorses.

He bought a top class thoroughbred Stallion called Denmark. He allowed it to be used on local mares, producing many good strong foals, and was thus a great influence in raising the standard of horses in West Cornwall

A fox as a visitor

Colonal Paynter loved riding with the Hunt as did his daughter Betty who rode side-saddle. Both were brilliant riders. George Aukett relates the following:-

One day seated at dinner I saw a fox racing for its life across the lawn. Presently the hounds and huntsmen and field in full cry galloped towards the house. The huntsman asked me if I had seen the fox, I replied "Yes, I saw it pass by the passage door". He made a search with the hounds and came back discomforted and said to me "I cannot imagine what happened to that fox". The hounds and field were formed up on the lawn when I was told by the Colonel to take them out refreshments and cigars. When these had been consumed I made my way to the scullery. By this time Hounds and huntsmen had disappeared. To my great astonishment when I arrived there, whom did I see but Mr. Reynard who had

71

THRESHING DAY at Boskenna Home Farm

evidently been able to observe all that had transpired from the scullery window! I immediately shut the window and the door, and sending for the gardener requested him to bring his dog and Mrs. Paynter's little dog "Susie". We then had a fox-hunt all on our own! Some time after, the master of the Hunt, Col. Bolitho requested me to show him the place where the fox took refuge, and was much amused.

FLOWER PICKING Boskenna Cliff, Billie Carbis and others and DAFFODIL TIME, William Rogers, Hilda Bailey, Elsie Jane.

Public duties.
Col. Paynter worked tirelessly for the community and was elected Chairman of West Penwith District Council in May 1925.

COL. PAYNTER'S THANKS.

(from the Cornishman 13 May 1925, abbreviated).

"Col. Paynter thanked the members very cordially for doing him the honour of electing him Chairman of the Council. Perhaps it would be too optimistic in a successor to office to expect that the mantle of his predecessor would fall upon him, but he would use his utmost endeavours during his term of office to maintain the traditions of the chair. He concluded by saying, common sense, mixed with a certain amount of goodwill, would enable water to be laid on to many hundreds of houses in the district, and they would hear less and less of the village pump with its concomitant expense and trouble.

"When I was in the army," concluded Col. Paynter, *"We had a brief and simple grace before dinner. It was 'God save the King and bless our dinner,' and I will conclude with a simple paraphrase of that: 'God save the King and bless our Council meetings in the coming year."*

He was a member of the County Council, and a magistrate for many years. In 1929 he became High Sheriff of Cornwall, a great honour! As Chairman of Newlyn Pier and Harbour Commissioners he did much to improve the harbour there.

Mrs Paynter dies

Mrs Paynter died on the 7 February 1933 after a short illness .Her coffin was brought to St. Buryan church on Colonel's lorry. The schoolchildren lined the pavement outside the school as the cortege passed. She was buried at her own request in a private enclosed grave near the sea at St. Loy. She was the first to be buried there. Second was her little dog named Sue buried at her feet. Third, the Colonel, and fourth, the ashes of Hugh Paynter.

Joyce Osborne daughter of the head gardener William Henry Penrose remembers the coffin of Mrs Paynter, plain oak with iron handles, being brought down in the estate lorry driven by Reggie Nicholls. Joe Tommy Warren, the St. Buryan schoolteacher, built the wall around the grave in the school holidays. I understand that Col. Paynter's granddaughter Sonya retained the ownership of the plot after the estate was sold.

Christmas Parties at Boskenna

An exciting event each year for the children of tenants and staff was the invitation to a Christmas party at Boskenna. They had party games and tea, and later under the Christmas tree Betty handed out presents, little dresses sometimes for the girls. Alice Grenfell supervised, and on occasion Mildred Angwin played for the games. These parties were held regularly until 1939.

LAMORNA BIRCH AND HIS DAUGHTERS by Laura Knight. (by permission University of Nottingham)

Chapter 10

BETTY PAYNTER

Elizabeth Narcissa Marie Paynter or Miss Betty, as she was affectionately known, was born in London on the 7th April 1907 the only child of Camborne Haweis and Mrs. Ethel Paynter She was christened at St. Peters, Eton Square. Soon after they returned to Cornwall.

At Boskenna she grew up to be a very lively child who knew what she wanted! What a wonderful life it must have been for her - surrounded by servants, a big house, lawns and gardens, trees and flowers, and the seashore, reached through flowery glades, a quarter of a mile away, peacocks on the lawn, and a horse or pony to ride. When she wanted to sow sweet peas she would read about it, how it should be done, and then get one of her father's gardeners to do it for her, but what she needed most was more company of her own age.

She was taught by a governess and in 1914, when she was 7 years old, she wanted someone to share her lessons. The artist Lamorna Birch had two girls, Mornie aged 10 and Joan aged 5. Their tutor Miss Burch had gone to join the household at St. Buryan Rectory. It was agreed that the two girls would come to Boskenna for lessons, and in return once a week Betty would come down and have painting lessons with Lamorna Birch. There were certain misgivings on both sides, as Mornie was at first frightened of Betty. Betty envied her having a little sister for company. For three years they had lessons together, the two girls arriving in the Lamorna pub jingle with Albert the pony, and returning in the Boskenna horse and trap. An oil painting, by Laura Knight, of "Lamorna Birch and his daughters," gives a good picture of what Mornie and Joan were like at that time. In 1917 Mornie went to boarding school but they remained lifelong friends. Betty also soon went to a boarding school in Bournemouth. Later Mornie was known as the artist Lamorna Kerr. A glamorous painting of Betty was always on view in her house.

BETTY PAYNTER aged 18

75

Famous visitors

Betty remembered as a child seeing Aleister Crowley holding a ritual in Trevellow Woods. *"We weren't supposed to be there not even as secret spectators . . .a real orgy fit for The News of the World!"* She tells some of her memories in 'Penzance to Lands End', a book by Michael Williams and John Chard, *"Lawrence of Arabia would roar up and down the drive on his motor cycle, and he was quite mad about my mother, Einstein would come over from Sennen when I was a small child and explain his complicated theories to me. D.H.Lawrence would come here from Zennor, Augustus John was a regular visitor, and one night he brought a baby that some young woman had given him. Father said "Leave it in the porch", but I went and deposited it in the kitchen with one of the servants. We had marvellous parties, it was not the thing to invite the 'trade' but artists were always welcome".*

Mrs.Estelle Fox remembers Betty wearing red velvet and riding side-saddle at horse shows. When she rode down to Lamorna to the Post Office Mrs.Trewhella used to give the horse sugar lumps. She often rode to Penzance on horseback and stabled at the Western Hotel. She changed in one of the bedrooms since her father would not have liked her walking around the streets in riding breeches. Betty said, *"The County used the Union Hotel in Chapel Street as a sorting office. We nicknamed it 'The Onion' and left our parcels there. Going home up Paul Hill with pony and jingle you got out and walked".*

Marconi of wireless fame

Guglielmo Marconi was a frequent visitor to Boskenna for four years or more up to 1925, with his 220ft. steam yacht Elettra anchored in Boskenna Bay.

Born in Bologna, Italy, in 1874 he showed an interest in making electrical gadgets in his back garden whilst a very young boy. His boyhood hero was Michael Faraday the scientist who made important discoveries in electricity and magnetism. Eventually after many painstaking experiments Marconi brought some of his results to be patented in England in 1896.

At Poldhu in south Cornwall Marconi built a high powered transmitter with aerials 200 feet high, from where he received the first Morse signal in 1901 the letter "S" from St. Johns, Newfoundland. Around the world the

MARCONI WITH BETTY PAYNTER

76

people were thrilled.

Perhaps his greatest success was in 1903 when the first two-way transatlantic wireless transmission was relayed. President Theodore Roosevelt sent a goodwill message from Cape Cod to King Edward VII, and from Poldhu greetings on behalf of the King were relayed across the Atlantic and picked up.

In 1905 he married a beautiful Irish girl Beatrice O'Brien.

By 1902 there were 70 ships equipped with Marconi wireless equipment and 20 land stations. This was done with great success. He was awarded the Nobel Prize in 1909. The imagination of the public was captured when, in 1910 wireless was used to capture the notorious murderer Dr. Crippin who tried to escape across the Atlantic on a passenger steamer. Wireless was also responsible for saving lives when the Titanic struck an iceberg in 1912. Many more would have been saved had the wireless operator on a nearby ship been on duty.

By 1912 Marconi had a son and a daughter. He and his wife Beatrice took a motoring holiday in Italy, and their car collided head on with another car and rolled over. Marconi lost an eye in the accident.

He became a member of the Italian Senate, and a diplomat, representing Italy at the Peace conference in Paris in 1919.

MARCONI WITH HIS TRANSMITTER

Elettra.

After the First World War he bought the Elettra a large ocean going 700 ton steam yacht from the British Navy. With a crew of 30 it was built for comfort and entertainment as well as a floating laboratory for experiments. It was originally built for the Archduchess Maria Theresa of Austria in 1904.

In 1920 he was on board his yacht in the Bay of Biscay making experiments in long distance radio reception, whilst his guests were dancing to live orchestral music from the Savoy in London!

Why so much about Marconi? In spite of being so busy with his experiments and his political life, he spent a lot of time at Boskenna with his yacht in the bay. While experimenting with short wave radio at Poldhu he had been invited to Boskenna with Capt. Lauro of the yacht Elettra. He installed a Supermarine wireless in the schoolroom, and local people marvelled that he could communicate with the Elettra while it might be travelling to Lamorna or even Falmouth. During the Great Strike of 1926, and other events of national importance, Aukett the butler, at Boskenna would take down notes from the wireless which the family would read with great interest. Ethel Paynter, Betty's mother was the first woman to speak to Australia by wireless. This was from Poldhu at the invitation of Marconi while he was doing experiments there.

One day Jack Ley, working for Col Paynter, drove Marconi to the Lizard.

Nearing there Jack spotted a lady whom he knew and suggested to Marconi that they pick her up. He agreed providing she sat in front. When she alighted she offered Jack the equivalent bus fare of one penny, which he refused. Marconi pocketed the coin instead!

ELETTRA Marconi's steam yacht

Romance

During his visits Marconi formed a strong attachment to Betty Paynter although she was much younger. His yacht was even seen around Bournemouth when she was at boarding school there. When she was 15 he gave her diamond bracelets and ruby rings which she had to hide from her teachers and parents. She was striking, athletic, and flamboyant, and possibly inherited some of her dark looks from an Indian great grandmother, Canon J.O.W.Haweis' mother-in-law. When Betty entered a room her personality was such that conversation would stop for a moment.

The artists at Lamorna were not all in favour of this attachment. Some thought of him as a woman chaser and vulgar, but not Lamorna Birch who was happy to attend receptions on the Elettra. On one occasion he rowed one of Marconi's women friends who was staying at Lamorna out to the ship. In 1924 Marconi and his Irish wife decided to separate.

Mediterranean Cruise

That autumn he invited Mrs. Paynter and Betty to a Mediterranean cruise on his yacht. This pleased Mrs. Paynter, (a long time friend of the inventor), who had ambitions for her daughter to marry him. What an experience for Betty sailing in the Med!. In an interview later she tells of Marconi taking her to meet the King and Queen of Spain and the King and Queen of Italy. They also visited Beruit and Damascus on their three months tour. Mrs Paynter took with her as lady's maid Chrissie Rowe, later Mrs.Will Pengelly of Burnewhall.

Christmas that year found Marconi back at Boskenna, and he and Betty attended a ball together at Penzance. In early April 1925 the national newspapers were predicting Betty's engagement to Marconi. He landed at the Prince of Wales pier Falmouth on Easter Saturday April 11th. On Sunday with Capt. Lauro he motored down to Boskenna. The Daily Express correspondent reported that they had a warm welcome from Mrs. Paynter. Betty and Marconi wandered off into the gardens. As the correspondent made his exit he met Col. Paynter returning from church. Col. said there was no engagement at present, that it was the ladies' affair, and he was leaving it with them. After lunch Betty dashed off into Marconi's car and they drove away laughing happily. What happened next? Perhaps we will never know. On Monday April 15th the St. Buryan Races were held. Betty, who was President, was present without Marconi. Next we read that the Elettra is in dock in Penzance, that Marconi is unwell and will not be giving interviews. (My friend Bob Rogers remembers seeing the Elettra in dock there). On the Thursday morning Marconi boarded the Cornish Riviera train to London and Betty and Capt. Lauro came to the station to see him off. The Captain was to sail the Elettra around to London to meet him after Marconi had seen some doctors. That day also we read in the West Briton 'The Press Association has received a message from Col. Paynter stating, *"Please contradict statements in the Press that my daughter, Betty Paynter, is engaged to Senator Marconi"*. It was also reported that when the Western Hunt next met at Boskenna Col. Paynter drove reporters out with a whip! Betty said Marconi lavished her with presents and wrote her letters and later proposed to her. *"There was no sex between us, and though he was a very sweet and generous man, the age was too great"*.

Why was Col. Paynter so annoyed? Was Marconi an ailing man? (He had been unwell coming up from Gibralter before Easter and again after). Did Betty break off the engagement? Did Mussolini and the Fascists put pressure on him? (He was very pro-British and even had a permanent suite at the London Savoy Hotel.) He once said, referring to his position as Senator, *"Don't ask me if I am proud of what I am doing!"* He never came back to Boskenna. He married again in 1926. On Tuesday 20th July 1937 he was sent for by Mussolini. That day he had a heart attack and Mussolini came to see him. He died in the night and four days later Betty was married!

79

Friends

In a lighter vein, I recall once talking to the Evergreen club at St Buryan on local history. I mentioned about Miss Betty's friendship with Marconi, and how they had dined at Buckingham Palace. One old man remarked, *"Marconi was very friendly with her mother too. you know"*. Perhaps we should take that with a pinch of salt.

THE GARDEN OF THE LITTLE BUDDHA, BOSKENNA. Painting by Lamorna Birch (by permission Christies Images)

Marconi's Parrot

At Boskenna there was a very mischievous grey parrot with an unprintable vocabulary. At first when he came he could speak Italian, as he was a gift from Marconi. One day, so I've heard, Violet Nankervis was going backwards down stairs sweeping. The parrot's cage was near the foot of the stairs and as Violet came near he leant out and gave her a great peck on the behind. She screamed, and the parrot jumped up and down flapping wings and cackling gleefully.

MORNING FILLS THE BOWL (LAMORNA). Painting by Lamorna Birch (by permission of the Royal Cornwall Museum)

81

I think the staff had fun training it for when Jack Ley waved his hat at the parrot it would screech *"Jack Ley you beggar, "* or words to that effect!

Michael Nicholls of Trevedran told me that during the War his mother would, (once a week), make butter at Boskenna. While she was thus engaged he would be left to his own devices and he, a four year old, would tease the parrot with a stick. I do not know how long Betty kept the parrot, but there is a story of her parrot being thrown out of a window in his cage into Chapel Street Penzance during an argument.

Betty Presented at Court

After cruising in the Med. in the autumn of 1924 with Marconi, and in the limelight with him at Easter, she was again in the spotlight as one of the 'debs' of the year in the summer of 1925. This meant being 'Presented at Court, and 'doing the London season'. With her mother as chaperon she would attend numerous parties, and would be introduced to suitable eligible young men. This was a 'marriage market' and 'debs' were expected to at least get a proposal of marriage in that year. The social round included: Queen Charlotte's Ball where the 'debs', perhaps 150 of them, wearing long white dresses, and after a fanfare from the band, would parade down the broad staircase in twos and on to the ballroom floor, a Private Viewing of the R.A.Summer Exhibition, Henley Regatta, Royal Opera, Windsor Horse Show, Chelsea Flower Show and much more. The cover picture is of the Paynters when Betty was presented at Court.

For Betty all this was very exciting. She had of late moved in 'high society', but she was brought up in what some would call 'a quiet backwater' at St. Buryan among country folk and her horses. For her friend Lady Swinfen (Mary Wesley), who was presented at court a few years later, it would be less exciting for she lived in a more sophisticated world.

Mia Kennedy, a close friend of Betty's, wrote *"When Betty was young she had a good life. She went out to India taking her horses. She was an excellent Polo Player, she played in the U.S.A. and the U.K. She played polo at Hurlingham when staying at her Chelsea flat in London. She was a very skilled horsewoman and took part in many equestrian events. She had spidery fingers and her wrists were the strongest of anyone I have known. Betty was a 'character', she always made an indelible impression. She was always capable of great kindness. I was very fond of her"*.

Prince of Siam

Among Betty's friends was Prince Beira the Prince of Siam, a polo player, an expert motor racing driver with his own team. He also had a biplane with canvas wings and a radial engine. One day flying to Boskenna he ran out of petrol landing in a field near Lissadel, St. Buryan. Jack Collins tells me he was a boy at the time

and as he approached the plane a man jumped out of it and, for a joke, chased him. He, thinking it was the Prince of Siam, was terrified and ran for his life.

Another friend of Betty's was Prince Chula a cousin of the Prince of Siam. His wife Princess Chula, an English lady was well known in Cornwall in later years for her public work. The two Princes were grandsons of the King of Siam.

Graham-White aviator
With the distinguished aviator Graham White, Betty claimed to be the first person

BETTY'S PARROT and ETHEL'S DOG

to fly to St. Mary's in the Isles of Scilly.

Recollections of David Evans
During the twenties and thirties, the Boskenna Estate was going downhill. It was a small landed estate by up country standards, and there was just not enough income from the tenanted farms to re-invest and keep the place going. Other landowners in England were tending to take land in hand as tenants died off, and farm it themselves, which was to become more profitable than having tenants, and was really the only means of survival for an estate. The Boskenna farms were all small units, and this would have been difficult. The Paynters' approach was progressively to sell off houses and land to obtain money to live on, which ultimately caused the break up of the estate.

Betty, who was about my mother's age, was asked to be my brother's godmother when he was born in 1934, although a more unsuitable person as a godmother, I can't imagine! He was later a page at Betty Paynter's wedding to Olaf Poulsen in 1937.

There seems to have been a young and rather fast set of "hangers on" - friends of Betty's, at Boskenna, during the thirties. One called Gyn Hancock, who was an out of work actor, as far as I remember, and several others. On one occasion Betty asked my mother if she would join her and some friends going to

FAMILY GRAVE

83

Hong-Kong. My father would have none of it!

Her behaviour could at time be outrageous. The Colonel restricted her telephoning activities at Boskenna, due to spiralling telephone bills, and since she was always short of money, she would descend on her friends. Coming to our house one day she said to my mother, "Oh, Joan darling, could I just make a very quick telephone call?" - It wasn't; it was a very long one and when the telephone bill subsequently arrived, my father discovered that it had been to Hong-Kong!

People loved Betty. Her charisma, her kindness, her humour, her eccentricity drew others to her. An example of this is in an incident that happened a few years later.

June Horn who had been on the Boskenna staff, was very close to Betty in her later years, She said *"I have many happy memories of her. None more so than as a passenger in her car driving in Market Jew Street, Penzance when she decided to park outside 'Peasgoods' the chemist blocking the road. A policeman appeared and asked if I would remove the car. Unfortunately I couldn't drive. When Betty eventually appeared she threw her arms around the policeman and said 'Darling how lovely to see you'. He replied 'How lovely to see you mam'! opening the car door for her. This sums up the great charisma Betty had."*

Miss Betty's wedding day

The sun shone brightly and great interest and excitement mounted in the ancient village of St. Buryan on Saturday 24th July 1937. Villagers and well-wishers jostled and crowded along the roads, and around the entrance to the church to greet the bride, Miss ELIZABETH NARCISSA MARIE PAYNTER, only child of COLONEL C.H. PAYNTER and the late Mrs. PAYNTER of Boskenna, St. Buryan, on the occasion of her marriage. The groom was Mr.M. OLAF POULSEN de Baerdemaecker of Chateau Hemelryck, Ghent, Belgium.

His family owned one of the oldest private shipping firms in Belgium, and he was grandson of Olaf Poulsen, the famous Scandinavian playwright.

The beautiful wooded valley of Boskenna was the setting three days previously when, early in the day, the Boskenna Staff was entertained to a special lunch, after which Mr. Aukett, on behalf of the staff, presented a silver teapot to the delighted Miss Betty.

A reception for members of the St. Buryan Women's Institute was held in the afternoon, tea being served. On behalf of the members, Mrs.R.M.Favell, President of the St. Buryan W.I. thanked Miss Betty for her kind hospitality, and wished her and husband-to-be every happiness. The presentation of an elegantly bound blotting pad, was made by the oldest and youngest members of the W.I. Mrs. Ramshaw and Miss N. Williams. In her thanks Miss Betty referred to the ladies of the W.I. as among her best friends and remarked that her grandmother had been very much involved in the infancy of the W.I. in the district.

BETTY PAYNTER marries OLAF POULSEN 1937

BETTY'S BRIDESMAIDS

Later in the evening at the presentation ceremony of the tenants and ex-tenants made by Messrs N.J.Hosking and G. Prowse, Miss Betty was pleased to receive a dressing case and a silver salver. Mr. Vivian Care presided at the ceremony.

To her mother-in-law Miss Betty gave a cut topaz and amethyst necklace, and some broad gold bracelets for the female members of the Boskenna staff.

During that day over 300 presents received by Miss Betty were on view along with her trousseau and wedding cake.

For 24 hours, led by Mr. Paull Hill and Messrs Hollow, florists of Penzance, the floral decoration of the church went on. Hundreds of blue and white hydrangea and colourful roses with greenery were the main feature, and about 20 men worked tirelessly through the night to ensure the scene was set for the great day.

CUTTING THE CAKE

For an hour the guests, dressed for the occasion, poured into the church. There were friends from overseas, representatives of famous English families, lords and ladies, generals and colonels, artists of note, magistrates and county councillors, close relations and friends, villagers and staff, almost 400 guests.

The summer sunshine filtered through the windows as the bride, escorted by her father, walked up the aisle to join her bridegroom at the altar, the organ playing "The Wedding of the Rose." She wore a long pearl satin gown, with a sapphire clasp given her by her mother, and her long pearl tulle veil was edged with gold thread. Her beautiful bouquet was made by Mrs. Constance Spry, who had been responsible for the bouquet carried by the Duchess of Windsor. It had been brought down in an aeroplane to Boskenna by Lord Sempill, famous airman and friend of the family. Some other guests also arrived by aeroplane.

The bridesmaids, Tania Vinogradoff, Jenefer Holman, Jenefer Fleming, Camilla Mulock, Daphne Douglas-Pennant, Elizabeth Williams, and Denise Harvey, were charmingly attired in pale blue organdie dresses, and little flower caps, and carried bunches of white flowers. The charming little pageboy was Tim Evans.

Local young girls, prettily dressed, Mildred and Betty Penrose, Barbara Williams, Margaret Williams, Alice Grenfell and Pam Hosking, Kathleen and Margaret Friggens carried rose petals in baskets. These they showered on the red carpet in front of the bride as she walked from the church. Margaret later had a 'bride' doll dressed in remnants of the same materials as Betty's outfit!

The best man was Herr H Gerhardt, a German friend of the groom, and the chief usher was Mr. Magin Hancock. The other ushers were Lord Sempill, Capt.

(the TENANTS' PRESENTATION, VIVIAN CARE AND NORMAN HOSKING

R. Burberry, Capt. J. Lethbridge, and Messrs. Michael Williams, V.C.Buckley, (the author), A. Bradley, E.K.Tremaine, and Simon Bolitho.

The service was conducted by the Bishop of Truro (Dr. Hunkin), and the Rector the Reverend C.B.Crofts, with Mr. Willie Gilbert at the organ.

A full Church led by the choir sang "O Perfect Love" and "The King of Love my Shepherd is". The ceremony was most impressive.

The bride and groom walked under a white awning on a red carpet to the gate where they were showered with rose petals. They passed through a cheering enthusiastic crowd to their car which took them back to Boskenna for their reception. I was 10 years old at the time but I vividly remember the event to this day!

St Buryan British Legion members who formed a guard of honour at the church were Messrs. J. T. Warren, W. H. Young, G. Chellew, S. Trewhella, A. Mitchell, N. Jenkin, G, Jackson, G. Williams, P. Matthews, J. Male, T. Bailey, V. Lugg, G. Quick, B. Lugg, J. Collins, R. V. Care, C. Lugg, W. Thomas, F. Hosken, R. J. Gilbert, R. Ash, J. Chapple, E. O. Murley, and J. E. Penrose. At Boskenna the Western Hunt was there to welcome them. The guests were received by the Dowager Lady Swaythling (standing in for the late Mrs Ethel Paynter), and

Colonel Paynter. The festivities ended with a dance held at the Tregenna Castle Hotel.

Donald Jarvis recalls that there was a tremendous amount of champagne drunk at the wedding, and he and Jimmy Galloway also celebrated in their own way when they found four full bottles thrown out with the empties!

George Aukett retires.

For George Aukett the butler it was also an important day. He wrote "The Day of days was favoured with glorious weather, resulting in the ceremony being witnessed by a tremendous concourse of people; the Church being filled to overflowing, large numbers were unable to enter". After describing the events of that day he concluded by writing, *"My own feelings were mixed, it having become necessary by reasons of ill-health for me to sever my connections with the household, and that, after 60 years of happy service and recollections; but I carried away with me the goodwill and wishes of many friends of long standing in St. Buryan and the neighbourhood".*

George had been happily married to Georgina Tonkin of a Methodist preaching family from Truro and was a widower for many years.

He was a man liked and respected by all with whom he came into contact, and worked for Col. Paynter at Boskenna as a butler and friend for 52 years or more, and before that was in the service of Colonel's grandfather Canon Haweis of Slaughham. It was there that George Aukett met the colonel and his brother, then in their teens, and heard of Boskenna, a gentleman's estate in Cornwall, which Master Camborne would inherit on attaining his majority. George was a talented musician and singer and was in demand at parties both at Lamorna for the artists, and at Boskenna when they were entertaining guests, 'a second George Robey' they called him! He also played cricket for Sussex I have been told.

The honeymoon

For their honeymoon Betty and her husband went by car to London, then flew to Scandinavia, their car to be sent on. Later they planned to visit Budapest.

Boskenna Deux

Donald Jarvis recalled the following:- *"After Betty and Poulsen had their honeymoon , I returned to Belgium with them as house man, with tail coat and red waistcoat. Their house was named Boskenna Deux, It was at Deurle 12 miles from Ghent. The house had four main bedrooms plus servants quarters, and the housekeeper, Berta, taught me French. Betty lived a life of leisure and social entertaining, and had staying with her an impoverished Austrian Countess and a large dog. She taught me to drive, and that could be hair-raising, as did flying with Poulsen in the fog.*

Poulsen managed a shipping company. His parents, who had started the

BOSKENNA DEUX, Betty's new home in Belgium.

business, lived at Chateau Hemery, a very big house with a large staff.

The War came and eventually Betty left Belgium. I stayed on, and when Boskenna Deux was commandeered we went to live in the Chateau. When the Germans broke through, Poulsen and I headed for Ostend with other refugees. We booked into an Hotel, but had to sleep in the wine cellar because we were being bombed. Next day we joined a boat sailing for England. We never saw each other again. I was called up, and Poulsen died in 1942 skiing or climbing possibly working for the 'underground movement".

OLAF POULSEN and his AEROPLANE

Chapter 11

WARTIME AT BOSKENNA AND AFTER

The second World War brought changes at Boskenna. Marketing of flowers had been big business on the estate, but as flowers were a luxury item they were not permitted to be transported by road or rail, to the markets up country. Early potatoes continued to be grown, but it was tedious work. Much of the cultivation, planting, and harvesting was done with hand tools. From some steep meadows even the potato sacks had to be carried up by hand, without the help of the young fit men, as many of the staff were called up for active service. Wages and other costs were escalating.

They employed land girls and one of them Janie Nicholls was milking cows with her brother Gerald helping her. He saw lots of rats in an old building. He and his brother Harry with dogs caught and killed a large number of them. When Colonel heard of it he called them up to the House saying "I give you the freedom of Boskenna!"

Betty comes home, wartime at Boskenna

Betty came home and her baby Diana Fleur Sonya Poulsen was born in November 1940 in Penzance. An early visitor was Norman Hosking from the Home Farm who brought baby Sonya a gold sovereign. Phyllis Prangnell made and presented to her a smocked dress. There were other presents. This was a big occasion for Boskenna which had so rarely heard the patter of little feet in the last 100 years .

Lady Swinfen (Mary Wesley the author) went to live at Boskenna with her two boys Roger and Toby. She had been a frequent visitor before the war, and left there in 1945 when the war was over. There were a lot of evacuee children there at different times too.

There were others: Alec Beechman our M.P. was often there, and Betty, nee Penrose a nanny, was often called upon to do office work for him.

The staff at Boskenna named it Hospitality House because some members of the armed forces convalesced there, including a RAF pilot who was badly burned.

Col. Paynter, who was 75 when war broke out, was head of the ARP in St. Buryan. Original members included Frank Hosken senior, William Henry Penrose, Harry Jane, and Enoch Prowse. Their duties included checking that no lights were showing, reporting the position of any bombs dropped, etc. Colonel gave encouragement to the Red Cross cadets, and their leader Dolly Stone. He was always kind to young people. I remember him as school manager visiting our primary school. He loved to hear the children singing, and would have the younger ones sing "Jesus wants me for a sunbeam".

He enjoyed presiding over events such as the Silver Jubilee and Coronation celebrations in 1935 and 1937 and Welcome Home for the Armed Forces after the war. He also enjoyed chairing meetings at the chapels such as the British and Foreign Bible society. At the end of a meeting at the little chapel of Borah near Lamorna Mr.Vivian Care stood up and in a humorous way thanked him by saying "We have just been singing 'From sinking sands He lifted me' and tonight Col. Paynter has raised the collection! "

Stephen Paull Jewell Hill
Betty Paynter's first husband Olaf Poulsen died in 1942, and in 1947 she married Stephen Paull Jewell Hill a solicitor of Penzance.

The following stories were related to me of Paull Hill. Paull had a problem in wartime, in that he had flowers from St. Loy to sell. *City folk were eager to buy flowers, but wartime restrictions meant petrol could only be used to move essentials like food, NOT flowers. So he invoked the assistance of the American Army. The flowers would be packed in wooden or cardboard boxes, clearly labelled LETTUCES. An American army truck would arrive under cover of darkness, often with a Negro driver. Paull, who had inside knowledge of such things, would instruct the driver carefully which route he should take out of Cornwall to avoid police road blocks, the truck (a 3-tonner) would be loaded up with 'lettuce', and set off in the night for Birmingham or maybe London. The driver would say that, if anyone tried to stop him he would drive straight on; the police having no jurisdiction over the US army!*

Paull was stationed in Burma at one time during the war. One day his CO summoned him, 'Paull, you have a civil flying licence for 2-engined planes, do you not? Yes. 'So please would you take the Dakota to X airstrip for us?' Why me? Because it's mined and I dare not risk a real pilot!' Paull did as requested. He liked a challenge and obeyed orders.

Childhood Memories of David Evans
We now come to my own memories of Boskenna. The earliest ones are of children's parties when I was about four. The then Lady Swinfen (better known today as Mary Wesley, the novelist - The Camomile Lawn and others), stayed there for quite a time, with her children, Roger and Toby Eady. Roger became quite a chum of mine, and I remember a drinks party for a whole lot of grown-ups in the drawing room at Boskenna and sitting in a corner of the room in Roger's pedal car, of which I was very envious. My parents and the Swinfens were there, together with Betty and a whole lot of other people. The children were looked after by the firm but kindly Alice Grenfell, who was Betty's Nanny looking after Sonya. Alice was quite a character. The story goes, that she took over the care of

91

the Swinfen children having said something along the line of:- "Lady Swinfen, it is perfectly obvious to me that you are totally incapable of looking after your own children, so I think that I had better look after them for you"! (Alice, who is still with us, has very high standards. She later became nanny to Lady Swinfen's children, at their home, and they are still good friends).

During the war, petrol was very scarce, so buses were used a lot. Roger used to come down for tea with us at Lamorna. He would catch the bus at Boskenna Cross, and we would meet him at Lamorna turn or in the village. Similarly, I would sometimes be met off the bus at Boskenna Cross, to go and have tea at Boskenna. I remember having tea in the kitchen, presided over by Alice. There was a parrot in the corner whom someone had taught to say - "b..... off"! The Colonel always used to come in and talk to us. I remember that there was an open fronted cart shed not far from the front of the house, which had in it a very ancient standard Fordson tractor with no mudguards and cleated iron wheels; quite possibly one of the first to come over from the Cork factory in 1915. I wonder what became of that?

On one occasion, Roger came to tea on my birthday, but no one had told him that this was the case. Now, of course, he is a great and noble Peer of the Realm, and no doubt makes eloquent speeches in the House of Lords, but in those days he talked broad Cornish. "I didn' know twas your birfdy", he said. At that he thrust his hand into his pocket and pulled out two china Father Christmases, the things that you put on a Christmas cake, saying, " 'ere, 'ave one o' they"! He was a gentle good-natured boy and I remember liking him very much.

Another thing that I remember at Boskenna was the Walled Garden, which has recently been restored to its former glory. There was a splendid cultivated blackberry in it. Helen McCabe, who lives at Boskenna now, was told not so long ago by Mrs Jane, that she remembered one day the Colonel was in the Garden talking to Major Evans, while Tim and David Evans, behind their backs, were quietly picking and scoffing blackberries!

In those days, the Colonel used to drive himself around in a rather battered olive green Ford ten. One day he went to sleep at the wheel and I remember my father coming home and telling us what had happened, and that John Henry Trewern from Trewoofe, had found him, with the car on its side, and had turned it back up onto its wheels again, single handed! He didn't drive again after that, and used to be chauffeured by Muriel Jackson from St Buryan.

He used to take Sonya and me to the Pantomime in Penzance over several years, to see Frank Barnes and Elizabeth Gilbert at the Pavillion. He was, in my mind a very kind and generous person and didn't ignore children, although I did hold him rather in awe. He was very well read and spoke French fluently, although, it is said, with an appalling accent! I gather though that he could be quite cantankerous and difficult concerning negotiations over property, and many of the conveyancing agreements made by him in Lamorna have caused problems ever since. He was the perfect gentleman in his general behaviour, although after his wife, Ethel Paynter, died in 1933, his amorousness sometimes caused embarrassment to women! He was often badly dressed. Definitely a character and an eccentric!

Like a beetle

From THE LIVING STONES by Ithell Colquhoun *The ground-landlord was Colonel Paynter, whose family had owned Boskenna for many hundreds of years, and still owned much of the land about Lamorna. Strangely enough, the old Colonel, one of feudalism's last relics, had been the first person I met when I arrived in Cornwall for a week's holiday during the war. There were no taxis in Penzance station-yard, and as I was standing forlornly by the suitcase I was unable to carry, not knowing how I was to cover the three or four miles that separated me from Mousehole, a little old gentleman kindly offered me a lift. his bent figure looked to me rather like a beetle, but this may have been because of his clothes - a sort of tail-coat and a bowler green with age - reminded me of a beetle similarly attired which I had seen long ago in an illustration in a child's book. I afterwards discovered that this was the Colonel's habitual costume. But his beady eyes, down curving nose and dark wrinkled skin added to the illusion.*

Fires at Boskenna

In the 1940s at Boskenna there were three fires which might have had serious results.

1 Mary Wesley writes of a fire which was caused by Col. Paynter pouring paraffin on damp logs when his library fire would not burn. *"This was New Year 1940. It was I who telephoned the Fire Brigade. They were rather reluctant to come I remember"*, she said.

2 Les Collins tells of a fire in 1947 at Boskenna as snow was falling. One engine went up Trelew Hill and got stuck in the snow between St. Buryan and Boskenna Cross. Les took his engine up Chywoone Hill and arrived safely. The fire had started in several places and the police were called. Col. Paynter explained that a bird had come down the chimney and carried the fire around the room!

3 This fire was on the night of the Hunt Ball, and would have been around the New Year 1948 or '49. Guests were at Boskenna having dinner before going on to the Ball at Tregenna Castle Hotel, St.Ives. In evening dress and ball gowns the party was in a merry mood. The fire broke out between the library and the dining room, and went up to Betty's bedroom. There was a big fuss, lots of smoke and two engines attended. Mildred George, nee Penrose, went into the bedroom on her hands and knees to rescue Betty's furs. Mildred's sister, Betty Penrose, was waiting at table at that time; she remembers being sent to the dairy for milk, (all were thirsty after all the smoke), and being given something to drink which made her

drunk! Capt. Sparrow summoned the guests into the Hallway and blew on the hunting horn as a signal for them to leave for the Hunt Ball!

It is amazing how an happening can be so much exaggerated in the retelling. Michael Paynter of Hants. had heard that the fire brigade, with strict Methodists aboard, was summoned to this dinner party, and they let it burn because "twasn't nothing there but naked wimmin and bottles!"

Ghosts

Tom Paynter wrote that there are many ghostly tales that survived from before 1800.

There is the 'Brown Gentleman' in 18th century clothes who resembled the third Francis, and the painting of him showed him wearing a brown coat! He was last seen in 1948. When the maid went to shut up the library for the night, she found Francis sitting in her master's chair. Tom Paynter wrote, *'With pardonable agitation, she rushed upstairs to tell him. My uncle had little use for ghosts. "Offer him a drink and perhaps he'll go", he replied, and continued his preparations for retirement. However even he admitted there were sounds in the house for which he could never account. He had grown used to them.*

There was a story that the Rockery was haunted, but Joyce Penrose with others watched and never saw anything! They told me that Lily Doble saw a ghost in the library two or three times, and that Lady Swinfen had seen a ghost, always a woman, several times. A wounded airforce man came to stay. He slept in the 'air-raid shelter', a downstairs room. One story says that in the morning he had gone, leaving a note saying he was too scared to stay any longer. Mr. Penrose remarked that he had probably heard the parrot.

Betty remarries

In 1947 Betty married again, this time to Stephen Paull Jewell Hill, a member of the Penzance firm of solicitors, and they lived in a cottage at St. Loy on the estate. The M.P.Alec Beechman was a guest at the wedding, and, I have been told, had wished to marry her himself.

Boskenna can be a lonely place, being at the extreme end of Cornwall and away from a town or village. Colonel's ancestor James found it so in his earlier years, and John most of his life. Colonel found it so during his last days. With Betty, her husband, and Sonya having moved into a cottage on the estate, Colonel was often alone in this mansion apart from the staff. Tim Evans writes *"My parents described to me Sonya, Betty's daughter, acting as hostess for the Colonel from a very early age. Betty seemed to be abroad a lot of the time".* In his last days he was happier alone with Sonya.

He gave up driving in his later years as it had by this time become rather more dangerous than usual. (Years before when Colonel was driving a tradesman's boy

BETTY marries PAULL JEWELL HILL 1947

leapt off his bike on catching sight of him, and ran up the hedge dragging his bike after him when Colonel passed.. *"Foolish boy! Foolish boy!"*, he said, *"I've nearly run over him once already this morning!"*). Colonel also felt the need to economise, and his small Morris car was lacking a set of matching doors.

Nearing the end of his life he told his housekeeper one night he was dying. *"Nonsense"*, she replied, *"You'll be out of doors singing in a couple of days"*, and he was. She reminded him of what she had said. He replied, *"Swans always sing before they die"*.

Even so he had a youthful capacity for enjoyment. A few days before he died, still young at heart, he went to see the pantomime, "Cinderella", enjoyed himself enormously, and went a second time. Unfortunately he caught a chill and did not recover.

Death of Colonel C.H.Paynter

Colonel Paynter died at Boskenna on 11th January 1949 just before his 85th birthday. His daughter Betty was summoned from London, and with his granddaughter Sonya were on the way to his bedside when he died.

95

At his funeral on Saturday 15th January the British Legion formed a guard of honour and school children lined the path to St Buryan Church. The service was conducted by the Rev.C.B.Crofts assisted by Rev.W.V.Wagner, vicar of Paul, who officiated at the interment in consecrated ground near the sea at Boskenna where his wife Ethel had been buried.

The coffin was taken on a flower decked lorry and ten estate employees acted as bearers.

How would one describe him? A fearless soldier and a clever man. He could speak in nine languages, and according to Sir Edward Bolitho, he could hold his tongue in all nine of them! He had a good sense of humour. His nephew also describes him as 'a great character, an excellent host, who had very many friends'. He loved children. Several have told me how he took them to the circus or pantomime .Ken Jeffery said "He used to take us children from Lamorna Church School on a trip to the circus by the old St Loy bus driven by Jack Ley, and provide us with tea. Quoting from the Cornishman, *"In every field of public endeavour he displayed a liberal-minded and progressive attitude. Newlyn is largely indebted to him for its improved harbour and it is no secret that he believed in paying his farm workers well and in giving them a Saturday half-holiday long before these measures had become common. He grew flowers on his beautiful estate and was always intimately interested in the land and the people who worked it.*

COL. PAYNTER and his grandaughter SONYA

Chapter 12

BOSKENNA, THE END OF AN ERA.

Ibiza

Mia Kennedy a close friend of Betty's wrote that they met when she arrived in Ibiza from Majorca in 1952. The following January she invited Mia to Boskenna and she stayed there in a cottage for 6 months. This pleased Betty who, like some of her ancestors, found Boskenna a lonely place, unless there were some visitors present. She would invite people to Sunday lunch usually 8 in all when she was home. Betty spent much of her time in Ibiza up to 1958. She called herself Betty Paynter Hill.

Battle of Lamorna

For those readers who have not been there Lamorna is a beautiful tree-lined valley which in spring is covered in a carpet of flowers, daffodils, bluebells, and primroses, with a stream that flows through it to the sea. At the mouth is a breakwater part of a tiny harbour where small fishing boats tie up.

Into this idyllic scene in the early part of the century came some famous artists to paint, and the Colonel encouraged them by erecting studios, garages, and some houses for them in Lamorna Valley

This was on the Lands End side of the Lamorna river. The other side was owned by Lord Falmouth and Lord St.Levan where there was very little development for housing, but over 100 years ago there had been much quarrying.

As the years went by keeping up Boskenna Estate became more and more difficult. Taxation, higher wages, and diminishing returns all took their toll, and Colonel Paynter had been very aware of it in his latter years. When he died the burden fell on Betty together with her husband Paull Hill. Death duties on Colonel's estate of £33,000 seemed the last straw!

Betty sold the Cove at Lamorna to Mr.John Daniel in 1953.

In 1954 the tax man insisted that she must sell the three farms at Trevedran, which she did to Mr Stephen Nicholls. At the end of 1954 in order to overcome financial difficulties Betty and Paull produced a plan to erect 126 houses, a petrol filling station, and a four acre permanent caravan site for 100 caravans at Lamorna. It caused such a furore in the community. Even her cousins and friends publicly opposed the plan. It was turned down by West Penwith District Council, Penzance Town Council, and the County Planning Authority.

A modified scheme was submitted withdrawing the caravan site and the petrol filling station, but requesting permission to put up 20 or 23 solid pre-cut timber houses with tiled roofs.

In order to test out the sincerity of the objectors, on December 6th Paull Hill (on behalf of his wife) offered to sell them the land for £17,500 which was considered by the Hills to be a little more than half its true value.

The following is copy of the last paragraph of a letter written to The Times on 11 Dec. 1954:

LAMORNA VALLEY

More than 60 years ago artists settled at Lamorna; many famous men found inspiration there; and to many visitors both from home and abroad, its beauty and interest have given delight. We, the signatories, beg that possible destruction of this unique and lovely valley should have your kind and earnest consideration. We are, Sir, yours &c.,

STANLEY SPENCER, W. REID DICK, FRANK DOBSON, CHARLES CUNDALL, A. R. MIDDLETON TODD, PHILLIP CUNNARD, W. MACMILLAN, W.RUSSELL FLINT, A.E.RICHARDSON, A. NEWTON, R.V.PITCHFORTH, FREDK. W. ELWELL, W.T.MONNINGTON, A.K. LAWRENCE, EDWARD MAUFE, LOUIS DE SOISSONS, MAURICE LAMBERT, HENRY RUSHBURY, JAMES FITTON, STANLEY ANDERSON, RUSKIN SPEARE, EDWARD LE BAS, RODERIGO MOYNIHAN, HENRY LAMB, GILBERT LEDWARD, STEPHEN GOODEN, ROBERT AUSTIN, J. BATEMAN, R.O, DUNLOP, ARNOLD MASON, JOHN NASH, ALFRED MUNNINGS, E.VINCENT, HAROLD KNIGHT, LAURA KNIGHT, REGINALD K. BRUNDRIT, GERALD KELLY.
Burlington House, Piccadilly, W.1.

A petition was signed by 113 people against the development, and a committee was elected to organise representation at the forthcoming Public Inquiry.

The committee elected: A.D.Izard chairman, F.Napper public relations, J.Collins treasurer, T.H.Chellew, D.Law, J.Small, L.Kerr, S.Hosking, and Major C.G.Evans, Mrs.J.Coward was co-opted as secretary, and Mrs.J.Small as representative of the Women's Institute.

Public Inquiry

The Inquiry took place at Penzance on 9.2.1955. A special bus was hired to take people living at Lamorna to St.John's Hall where they joined large crowds who had gathered there.

Mrs.Hill (Betty) was appealing against the refusal of the county planning authority to allow her first proposal, and her later modified amendment. She was represented by her husband Paull Jewell Hill. Among the official objectors was her first cousin Mrs.M.A.Dakin, (representing Paul Parish Council), and Colonel J.H.Williams (Elephant Bill).

Paull Hill said that from the outset Colonel Paynter had intended developing the village and cove. He had installed the water supply, and also kept the harbour in repair. He had built or converted a large number of houses, and had built a petrol station and garage in the centre of the village. Those owning the eastern side were opposed to the building of houses, but had opened three granite quarries and left thousands of tons of blocks still scattered about, making the greatest eyesore in the valley.

Paull Hill went on to tell of his wife having been faced with £33,000 death duties and having had to sell a number of properties.

Mrs.Hill (Betty) said Lamorna attracted "curious and wonderful geniuses" who to the Cornish people were foreigners. She felt most for the Cornish people who belonged to Lamorna. *"I love Cornwall and am paying for loving Cornwall"*.

Blood was no longer thicker than water, for her cousin, former County Court Judge, Scobell Armstrong, was to put the case for the residents opposing the scheme.

"I have no eloquence, but stand before you frightened and bewildered".

Among the artists called were Mrs. Lamorna Kerr and Mr.Charles Simpson.

Plan opposed, the curtain falls

Colonel had been a benevolent landlord. He had brought a water supply to Lamorna at considerable loss. He had improved the road to the cove, and maintained the harbour at his own expense. He had built studios and built or adapted houses as and when needed, and was a real friend of the Lamorna community and the artists in particular. He had built the Ark Garage for petrol and repairs, and a dairy and vegetable shop

Betty was trying to save her home and her estate even the jobs of many employees.

This was her property. At Lamorna Gate at the entrance of the valley her father, in earlier days, even had the gate there closed once a year to maintain his ownership of the road.

Why was everyone lining up to oppose her? Margaret Ann Dakin one of her nearest relations? Lamorna Kerr her dear friend? Gilbert Evans a dear friend of her father's and her friend too? Nothing had really changed. People still loved Betty and cared about her, but they also cared about the future of Lamorna

Mr.S.P.B. Mais in his book on the Cornish Riviera wrote of Lamorna: Everything here seems to have been touched with a magic hand.

Lamorna is a unique place and to have built 126 houses there would have destroyed what is irreplaceable.

With the failure of planning approval for Lamorna it was the end of the road for the Boskenna estate.

WEST CORNWALL
The Valuable, Freehold
AGRICULTURAL ESTATE
known as the
BOSKENNA ESTATE
in the Parish of
SAINT BURYAN
containing some of the earliest Farm and Market Garden Land in the British Isles,
lying on the South Cornish Coast between Penzance and Lands End, comprising
SEVEN FARMS AND FIVE MARKET GARDEN HOLDINGS
Vacant possession of Boskenna Home Farm at Michaelmas
Vacant possession of four of the Market Garden Holdings
embracing a total area of
442 ACRES or thereabouts
and providing a rent roll of
£791 per Annum
the whole of which are to be offered for Sale by Public Auction
at The Central Auction Rooms
Morrab Road, Penzance, at 3 p.m. on
THURSDAY, 21st MARCH, 1957
Auctioneers W.H.Lane & Son, Penzance 2286

Lot 1 - The attractive Manor House (vacant) and Manor Farm.   £6,000
Lot 2 - Boskenna Nursery, three-quarter-acre glass. Vacant Possession.
Lot 3 - Boskenna Home Farm, 100 acres Vacant Possession Michaelmas.
                                                                    £8,450
Lot 4 - St Loy Cottage and Smallholding, 11 acres, Vacant Possession.
Lot 5 – St Loy Cottage and Smallholding, 11 acres. Sea frontage. Vacant
possession.   £1,750
Lot 6 - St An Dellan, cottage and 11 acres. Sea frontage. Vacant Possession.
                                                                    £2,250
Lot 7 - Boskenna Cliff.   £1,100
Lot 8 - Borah Farm   £2,025
Lot 9 - Boleigh Farm.   £1,750
Lot 10 - Clapper Mill Farm   £1,750
Lot 11 - Trewoofe Farm.)_   £5,500
Lot 12 - Trewoofe Farm)
Lots 8 to 12 comprise 5 tenanted farms
        Lots 2 and 4 were sold separately. The other 10 lots sold for a total of
only £30,575

Of Interest to Connoisseurs,
Collectors and Dealers.

BOSKENNA MANOR, ST. BURYAN,
WEST CORNWALL.

IMPORTANT SALE OF ANTIQUE
FURNITURE, PORCELAIN,
PICTURES AND OTHER OBJECTS
D'ART.

Comprising more particularly:—

Rosewood and inlaid Sheraton sofa table (5ft. x 2ft.); Rosewood and inlaid oval Pembroke table (3ft. 6in. x 2ft.); Rosewood and inlaid writing desk (3ft. 6in.); Sheraton Satinwood needlework table, 2ft. x 1ft. 3in.); Mahogany Chippendale Chinese table (4ft. 6in. x 2ft. 3½in.); Walnut and inlaid Folding Sheraton D. end card table (3ft.); Carved European walnut table (4ft. x 2ft. 9in.); Mahogany extending dining table with three leaves (11ft. 9in. x 3ft. 6in.); Walnut circular pedestal table 4ft. 6in. diam.) Three Mahogany pedestal tables; Walnut and inlaid Satinwood workbox; Mahogany Sunderland table (3ft. x 2ft. 6in.); Leather top writing desk (4ft. x 2ft. 3in.); Mahogany drop leaf dining table (3ft. 9in. x 4ft.); Oak gateleg table; Mahogany drop leaf dining table (4ft. 6in. x 2ft. 3in.); Carved oak hall chest with brass lock plate (4ft. x 1ft. 8in.);

Set of Six Mahogany framed Chippendale chairs and a set of Four similar chairs; Set of Twelve Mahogany Queen Anne vase back chairs; Mahogany framed wing armchair with brocade silk upholstery. Two Country Chippendale chairs; Carved oak stool with cabriole legs and claw and ball feet and tapestried upholstery; Mahogany stool with cerise upholstery; Queen Anne oak stool with zig-zag needlework top; Oak framed stood with upholstered seat and turned legs; Mahogany framed armchair with stamped red velvet upholstery; a settee with cerise covering.

Hepplewhite carved Mahogany four Poster bed (5ft.); Eight divans with Spring Interior Mattresses.

Brass Bound wine tub; Embossed tapestry firescreen; Two Victorian beadwork footstools.

Two moulded gilt framed mirrors; Walnut and gilt framed George I wall mirror; Georgian gilt framed convex mirror with two ormolu lights; Gesso wall mirror.

Baby Grand Piano by John Broadwood & Son; Long case clock in lacquered case by Benjamin Davis, London; French gilt ormolu striking wall clock; Mahogany bracket clock; French Boule work mantel clock; French Lyre clock.

Lacquered hanging corner cupboard; Carved Nubian pedestal; Mahogany Bow front tallboy (3ft.); Walnut dressing-table; 17th Century oak armorel (4ft. 6in.); Queen Anne Mahogany extending dressing-table (3ft. 3in.); Two Gent's Mahogany wardrobes; Hepplewhite Mahogany show cabinet; Mahogany cupboard chest (7ft. 3in.).

A Caucasian runner 10ft. x 3ft. 3in.); Red patterned carpet (16ft. 3in. x 14ft. 8in.).

Large quantity of family oil portraits including one of John Paynter by Opie; A pair of Bartolozzi prints of paintings by Sir Joshua Reynolds, R.A.

Library of books including "The works of Jeffrey Chaucer 1687"; "Borlases History of Cornwall 1754"; "Paxtons Magazine of Botany 1834-41"; "Cooks Second Voyage" Third Edition; and many other antique books and prints.

Oriental and European china and porcelain including a pair of Nailsea vases (15½in.); pair of Dresden monkeys (5in.) (imperfect); a Dutch Delft drug jar converted to table lamp; a Chelsea leaf shaped dish; pair of Bisque Sevres oviform vases and lids; Two Chinese armorial dishes; pair of Delft fluted cannisters; Twenty-one air twist early English glasses; English group of porcelain figures with floral brocade.

Several pairs of red stamped velvet and other lined curtains.

Quantity of household and kitchen utensils, china, cutlery and linen; and many other useful lots; also Allen Motor scythe with three 3ft. blades and power spraying attachment; Howard Bantam rotavator; Atco power power 24in.; circular saw bench; "Wizard Simplex" oscillator and 120ft. spraying line; Clifford plough; Goradam easy eight soil block maker; large quantity cloche glass; Goodwin concrete mixer; Ladders; flower pots; potato trays; Two wheelbarrows with rubber tyres.

Boskenna:- Sale of Furniture Antiques etc.
May 3rd 1957

Boskenna was sold to Dr.Thompson and his wife. Forty years on it is a joy to see the mansion and grounds so well cared for by the present owners, Gilbert and Helen McCabe.

The sale of Boskenna brought sadness to many. The end of a colourful era, the end of the saga of the Paynters of Boskenna. It is almost the end of my story. Betty moved to Penzance, but spent time elsewhere, London, Majorca, Ibiza, etc. Her daughter Sonya married in 1959 and had two sons Robin and William. As time went by Betty's financial situation deteriorated and by 1979 she was on very slender means. By this time she was living at Penrose Terrace, Penzance in a flat next door to her ex-husband Paull Jewell Hill.

From the newspapers of December 1979 it appears that a young man, who had been a close friend to Betty, had a drink problem. He tried to break in to her flat. The next day he died in hospital after being shot in the leg. Later Betty's husband was cleared of his murder.

The following Sunday Betty, dressed in black, attended mass at the Roman Catholic Church.

Betty dies

That winter Betty was a patient in St. Michael's Hospital, Hayle, and in the spring she went to Portugal to recuperate. She died suddenly on 10th July 1980 at the age of 73 and was buried there. A mass was held at Penzance Roman Catholic Church. Many times in her later years Betty must have longed for the days of long ago at Boskenna! Her wish had been to be buried there near her father and mother, but it was not to be.

One can still picture Col.Paynter, with head bent, toddling around the corner of the house, and Marconi and Capt. Lauro getting out of their limousine. Miss Betty riding up to meet them on her horse Bandon. Memories still pervade this place.

Sonya

Sadly I must add a postscript, for Betty's daughter Diana Fleur Sonya Menzies, died in London on the 8th December 1998 aged 58 years. There was a Memorial Service at St.Mary Abbot Church, Kensington at which a large number attended. Sonya left a husband, George, and two sons of her first marriage, Robin and William Paynter Bryant.

Sonya spent much of her first 16 years at Boskenna, the ninth generation to do so. It was fitting that Toby Eady, Lord Swinfen's younger brother, should give an eulogy, and take the mourners back to Sonya's early childhood at Boskenna where he and his brother were her constant companions. Mention was also made of

BETTY at 65 years

Dolphie Mitchell, an old St.Buryan 'character' who at times assisted them in their games. Present also were Paul Dakin and David Evans who also had spent many happy hours at Boskenna and knew her well. It was fitting that they were there to represent her many friends in West Cornwall.

Each generation of Paynters has contributed something to their county seat at Boskenna in some measure. Although many were at times absent, each exerted a certain influence for change; upon their family and the local community. Until the end of the last Great War changes were slow to affect the pace of life of "the gentry". After the war a new approach to estates, their employees, and their owners, quickly meant a situation of "no return" to the pre-war days, affecting the survival of several Cornish estates where financial burdens overtook them.

The Paynter family still evoke among the older folk great affection, loyalty, and respect. We mourn the passing of Sonya. She was the last of that old family to reside in the beautiful mansion of Boskenna.

The Paynters at Boskenna Hall
Two eighty years have been,
And in the flickering firelight
Remember them and dream.

APPENDIX

The Captain and Nellie
From a story in Bottrell's book
"Legends and Hearthside Stories of West Cornwall".

Carthew of Boskenna was quite a rake, and after him did his daughter take
And much troubled indeed was Mrs. Carthew, to make Nellie, like her - 'A lady too'.

Nellie wandered often down St. Loy, and met there one day a sailor -boy
Who from the Law had taken flight - he had killed a man in a proper fight.

At last this Billy Brea from Brea, with his cousin Bosvargus sailed away.
For three years on England turned his back, and was later known as Captain Black.

Meanwhile Nellie waited alone, long nights at St. Loy for her lover's return.
At last he came, to elope with her, and agreed to meet at St. Buryan Fair.

St, Buryan Fair was on a stormy night, but this did not lessen Nellie's delight
As she hurried up through wind and rain, to St. Buryan Church-town to dance again.

At the public-house there was such a life, with music from tambourine, violin, fife;
Captain Black had folks mesmerised, as he led the dancing unrecognised.

When for a time the storm died down, they went out and danced around the town;
Folk came from the houses to join them there, down to Pare-an-Cady and around the square.

Suddenly there was thunder, lightning, hail, and rain came down, as from a pail!
And as in fright the people cower, loud rang the bells up in the tower.

They thought the Captain was the 'Evil One', when he and Nellie, they found, had gone.
But the lovers sheltered, both weary and worn, in the old 'Downs Barn' from the mighty storm.

The barn caught fire but they got away, and were on the ship at break of day.
After them, too late, rode Squire Carthew, for they had set sail from Market Jew.

They got married when next ashore; then back again to sea once more;
And chased the Spaniards with might and main, which did for them much treasure gain.

So Nellie sailed before the mast, had many sons as time went past.
Some deeds were done which I daren't tell, and they all got rich on the Lovely Nell.

Passing the Cornish Coast one day, when twenty years had passed away,
Nellic saw once more Penberth and Treen, and longed to be at home again..

The Captain first would have sold his loot, but in Nellie such longing had taken root
At Falmouth he got for her a horse, and in haste she took the homeward course.

Sad news at St. Buryan when Nellie arrived, none of her family she found survived
Except Betty Trenoweth who now did reside, in St. Buryan village on Trevorgans side.

Betty told her, her Father was buried that day, but before that his wealth he had wasted away;
Then the mortgage came in the Paynters' hands,and now they are owners of his lands.

The Captain and Nellie gave up the sea, at Trevorgans bought some property.
With all their wealth they did retire, and he lived in style as a Country Squire.

Now the Captain had a roving eye, and Ackey Carne was a fool to spy
On Miss Tresillian with Captain Black, and soon had her family on his track.

Her family were powerful and did try, to make Ackey do penance and deny
At St. Buryan Church, as custom, clad, in sheet, and bare feet, this fearless lad.

To the Rood-screen he came, and without kneeling, he turned to the people and said with
feeling,
"Here am I, compelled by Law, forced to deny what mine eyes saw".

He went on to relate in language not choice, about what he had seen he quickly gave voice.,
The Captain at once the challenge took up, and out in the square unarmed they fought.

Long was the struggle, rough was the fray, both tired at last and called it a day,
O'er a bowl of punch they made amends, and afterwards were firmest friends.

The Captain soon tired of the 'landlubbers' way, and with Ackey went smuggling to Brittany.
Returning home in a fearsome gale, the Captain refused to shorten sail.

With lightning to show them to their berth, the terrified crew soon reached Penberth.
When they had landed their kegs of rum, they lit a fire and broached a drum.

When the carousal was at its height, they broached another which caught alight;
Suddenly the flames grew higher and higher, and the Captain and Ackey were burnt in the fire

Whether the Captain was the 'Evil One', or whether the man was daring, in fun,
To make a conjecture leave with you, but as far, as I know this tale is true.

(The Carthews had been living at Boskenna for about 100 years)

Boskenna Staff

Employment at Boskenna opened new vistas to members of its staff.

Jack Ley on the recommendation of Harry Payne was promoted from market gardening to mechanic and chauffeur, and 80 years on his family are providing a public service by running two garages. Some like Dorothy Yeoman, Christine Pengelly, and Alice Grenfell, travelled with the Paynters to London and other places.

The Paynter family received loyalty and support over long periods from their staff. In memory of them and for a historical record here are some of their names.

Staff who commenced worked before 1915

Men: George Aukett, (butler); John Collins, (engineer); John Henry Trewern, (he came there in 1900, at the age of 17, and worked nowhere else), chauffeur; William C. Lugg and John Jarvis, (carpenters); Tom Bailey, (coachman); Charlie Johns, (horseman); George Polgrean, (clerk); Johnny Williams, Will Stone, Dick Stone, John Warren Stone, D. Wood, Harry Payne, William Mill or Hill, Chris Jelbert, William Penrose, Harry Wharton, Jim Grenfell, Charlie Leah, Mr. Nichol, (fishery manager); Major Gilbert Evans, (agent);

Women: Nanny Hocking was cook at Boskenna until she left to get married in 1869. She was presented with a Bible and some inscribed plates.

Mrs Bannerman, (cook); Jesse and Amy Godfrey, Annie Marley, Mrs.Dunstan, Miss White, Miss Young, Mrs.Jinny Lugg, (she came from London with Mrs.Ethel Paynter 1904).

Those who commenced work there after 1915

Men: Dick Thomas, (mason), and Ernest Stone, also a (plumber); Percy Richards, (carpenter); Lional Ellis, (painter); Jack Ley and Reggie Nichols, (mechanics); Roland Morris, (who was later the famous diver. While much under age he offered and drove Marconi once to Poldhu), Harry Jane, Billie Carbis, (chauffeurs/lorry drivers); Harry Carbis, (groom); Dolphie Mitchell, (horse/tractor driver); Mr. Harry, William Henry Penrose, (head gardeners/foremen); John Keiser (butler), Tom Bailey, Arthur Trembath, Jimmy Galloway, Jack Lugg, Jack Collins, Douglas Penrose, William Rogers, (gardeners); Billie Penrose, Cecil Penrose, Will Tom Strick, Mr. Roskilly, Tom Nankervis, Jack Andrewartha, Will Strick, Jake Sibthorp, Alf Wilshaw, Charlie Berryman, Ted Chapple, Jimmy Grenfell, Jack Angwin, Aubrey Praed, Tommy Semmens, Geoffrey Rowe, George Ireland, Frank Strick, Peter Thomas, - Rudd, Laurence Hall, Jack Rogers, Owen Warren, Donald Jarvis, Cecil Carbis, Edmund Trewhella, Jimmy Clemens, Tommy Lugg, Billie Thomas, George Semmens, Johnny Flint, Freddie Phillips, Stanley Penrose, B.Ellis, Bob Batten.

Women: Alice Grenfell, (now in her nineties, she had many roles, but has always been loyal and wonderfully supportive, and is a dear friend of the family); Hilda Bailey, Mrs. Ethel Williams, Mrs.Jane, Winnie Grenfell, Lily Doble, Betty Penrose, Janie Hosking nee Angove, Chrissie Pengelly nee Rowe, Dorothy Yeoman, Lily Bailey, Lydia Strick, Helen Keiser, Janie Gartrell, Violet Nankervis, Norah Bassett, Mary Priest, June Nankervis, Roma Nankervis, Mollie Symons, Dorothy Berryman, Phyllis Prangnell, Elsie Jane, Leonora Simpson, Azure Trevaskis, Janie Nicholls, Mildred Penrose, Mrs.Flint, Muriel Jackson, (chauffeur).

For Colonel Paynter at Lamorna George Penrose ran a garage, served petrol, and hand milked 3 or 4 cows, while his wife ran Colonel's shop selling produce milk, eggs, fruit, and vegetables, much of which Colonel had brought fresh from Boskenna that day.

Most of these names and occupations have been suggested to me. There must be more, and many of those mentioned would have different kinds of work at different times in their lives.

'TREE' of MARY ANN CARE

WILLIAM 1770 - 1836
Farmed Boskenna Home Farm from about 1820

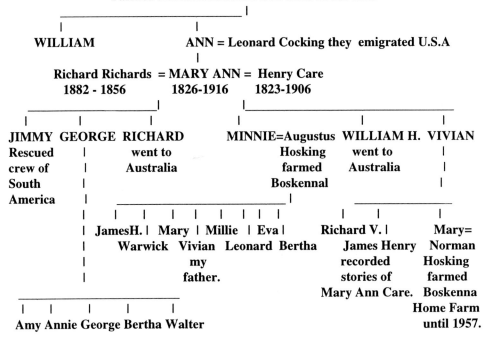

```
WILLIAM                    ANN = Leonard Cocking they emigrated U.S.A

            Richard Richards = MARY ANN = Henry Care
               1882 - 1856      1826-1916    1823-1906

JIMMY   GEORGE  RICHARD        MINNIE=Augustus  WILLIAM H.  VIVIAN
Rescued    |    went to            Hosking       went to      |
crew of    |    Australia          farmed        Australia    |
South      |                       Boskennal                  |
America    |                                                  |
           |    |    |    |    |    |   |    |    |    |        |
           |  JamesH. | Mary | Millie | Eva |   Richard V. |     Mary=
           |   Warwick  Vivian  Leonard Bertha   James Henry   Norman
           |              my                     recorded      Hosking
           |            father.                  stories of    farmed
                                                 Mary Ann Care. Boskenna
                                                                Home Farm
  |    |    |    |    |                                         until 1957.
Amy Annie George Bertha Walter
```

108

Boskenna

Nine verses from a long poem by Mrs S.E. Tonkin of Manchester, **1868**

Hail fair Boskenna! Mansion by the sea!
On fancy's wings I now return to thee;
Again I see thee, stately and serene,
Smiling in beauty, like a virgin queen.

Fair are thy ranks of lichen crisp'ed trees
That eastward turn from the Atlantic breeze,-
Soft is the moss that decks their leafy arms,
Outstretched o'er ferns that wave like mimic palms.

In gladsome thoughts my memory recalls
The peaceful hours spent in Boskenna's halls;
I see again her polished walls of pine,
Enriched with glories that envolumed shine.

E'en now 'tis rest to close the outer eye
And bask in memory of the western sky;
To tread with dainty step, as when of yore
We left Boskenna for the rugged shore.

Entranced I stand . Far as the eye can peer,
The waters roll, divinely blue and clear;
With white sails flashing in the sunlight's ray,
Of countless vessels, near and far away;

White 'neath Boskenna's cliffs the boulders lie,
And rocks titanic rear themselves on high
I must away; hid 'neath the rocks, and coy,
Boskenna's love lies sleeping-- fair St. Loy;

A pleasant ramble through a bosky vale;
A pause to hear a babbling brooklet's tale;
A moment's lingering by it's mossy well,
And I once more am in St. Loy's green dell.

Ages ago, as old traditions say,
The monks devout stole here to fast and pray;
Within these wilds they communed by the sea
And reared for worship a fair chapelry.

By devious pathways now I track the glade,
And soon regain Boskenna's green arcade,
Yet have I dreamed a happy dream and true,
I will not weave therein a sprig of rue.

ACKNOWLEDGEMENTS AND THANKS

My thanks go to so many people who have shown interest and helped with this book.

Here are some of them.

Paintings and Photographs

Tim & Jill Evans: Presentation at Court (cover picture); Ethel Nina Patience Paynter; Betty Paynter marries Olaf Poulsen; Cutting the cake.

Mrs Ryan: Trelissick.

Monica Tremayne: Boskenna Home Farm; Jimmy Richards & W.H.Care; Betty at 65.

Jack Collins: John Collins, George Aukett, Col. Paynter; Betty Paynter at 18.

Paul Dakin: Lieutenant Hugh Paynter; Kasuga Cruiser; Lieutenant Hugh Paynter being entertained in Japan; Trevellen Lamorna; Ann Dakin; Donnett Paynter.

Reproduced by permission of Adam Kerr: The Abertay, painting by Lamorna Birch.

Norman Hosking: Annie Johns with Mary Care of Boskenna Home farm; Tenants' Presentation.   Tony Praed: Jack Ley Jim Grenfell and others; Threshing day.

Reproduced by permission of the University of Nottingham: Lamorna Birch and his daughters, painting by Laura Knight, also permission of Austin Wormleighton (from his book: A Painter Laureate).

The Cornishman: Marconi with Betty Paynter

The Western Morning News: Marconi with his transmitter.

Sea Breezes: The steam yacht Elettra.

Reproduced by permission of Christies Images: The Garden of the Little Buddha. , painting by Lamorna. Birch, also permission of Austin Wormleighton (from his book: A Painter Laureate).

Reproduced by permission of the Royal Cornwall Museum, Truro: Morning fills the Bowl, Painting by Lamorna Birch.

Joyce Osborne: Betty's parrot, Family grave, Betty's bridesmaids, Col. Paynter and Sonya.

Donald Jarvis: Boskenna Deux; Olaf Poulsen and his aeroplane.

Steph Haxton: drawings

Other Material

Paul Dakin: Loan of A Parcel of Lawyers by Tom Paynter, and other material.

David and Tim Evans: for their recollections of Boskenna and the Paynter family.

Tricia Sanderson: Research of Hansard. Austin Wormleighton A Painter Laureate. Mary Siepman (Mary Wesley), Lord Swinfen, Adam Kerr, Alice Grenfell,. Gilbert and Helen McCabe, Douglas Penrose, Joyce Osborne, Jane Tweed, Donald Jarvis, James Henry Care, Clive Carter, Mia Kennedy, June Horn, Mary Warren (Newlyn), Gerald Nicholls, Winifred Treleven, Iris Warren, Hazel Hocking, Rev. Tom Shaw, The Cornishman, The Western Morning News, The Morrab Gardens Library and The Public Library Penzance, Cornwall Record Office, The Courtney Library, Cornish Local Studies Library, National Maritime Museum, Charterhouse School, also thanks to the many who filled in my questionnaire or provided other information.

I thank Nancy Wallis for proof reading, advice and encouragement.

My grateful thanks also to Douglas Williams for his excellent 'Forward' to this book

BIBLIOGRAPHY

A Parcel of Lawyers Tom Paynter
Some historical notes of Mary Davies Paynter
Notes on 60 years service with the Haweis and Paynter families, George Aukett
A Painter Laureate Lamorna Birch and his circle Austin Wormleighton
Summer in February Jonathan Smith
Penzance to Lands End Michael Williams and John Chard
The Living Stones Ithell Colquhoun
History of Penzance P.A.S.Pool
J.H.Care and his Childhood Memories J.H.Care
Patten People No.4 In Time and Place, Lamorna, by Elizabeth Lamorna Kerr and Melissa Hardie